# THE
# KILLER
# INSTINCT

# THE KILLER INSTINCT

## BOB COUSY

with JOHN DEVANEY

RANDOM HOUSE
NEW YORK

Library of Congress Cataloging in Publication Data

Cousy, Robert, 1928–
    The killer instinct.

    1. Cousy, Robert, 1928–   2. Basketball. 3. Basketball coaching.
I. Devaney, John, joint author. II. Title.
GV884.C68A34      796.32'3'0924 [B]      75-10279
ISBN 0-394-49469-5

Manufactured in the United States of America

# ACKNOWLEDGMENTS

This book began as an account of the way in which widespread cheating in the recruitment and support of players has damaged big-time college sports. To a degree the book is still about that subject, but it has also become the story of what the intense pressures of big-time coaching have done to one man—me.

John Devaney and I owe a debt of gratitude to Larry Lorimer, our editor at Random House, for conceiving the original idea and then guiding us as we traveled new roads. We were also aided by my former associates at Boston College, notably my former assistant, Frank Power, and sports information director Eddie Malone. Nick Curran, the director of public relations for the National Basketball Association, was kind enough to provide films that refreshed my memory of games I participated in as coach of the Cincinnati Royals and the Kansas City—Omaha Kings. And Joe Axelson and Larry Staverman were helpful in providing other material. Also of great help in giving us background on college athletics were Dee Rowe, basketball coach at the University of Connecticut; New York lawyer Lewis Schaffel; and Brendan Malone, coach at Power Memorial High School in New York.

To all, our thanks.

Bob Cousy
Worcester, Massachusetts
May 1975

For those who give a damn

# CONTENTS

# THE
# KILLER
# INSTINCT

# WINNING
# AND
# LOSING

It was April 1963. I had just arrived in Los Angeles with the Boston Celtics for the final game of the National Basketball Association championship playoffs. After thirteen years with the Celtics this would be my last game.

I walked into my hotel room and locked the door. For the next thirty-six hours I stayed inside that locked room alone. I ordered all my meals sent up. I talked to no one. I didn't answer the telephone. I thought so long and so intensely about Frank Selvy, the Laker guard I would be playing against, that if he had walked into that room I might have leaped at his throat and tried to strangle him. If anyone had touched me or even talked to me, I might have tried to kill him. Or, more likely, I would have broken down and wept.

The next day I ran onto the court to play for that championship with my insides as taut as violin strings, my throat too tight for speaking. Yet outwardly I appeared to be calm, almost daydreamy. My body was under rein, ready to function.

This state—controlled on the outside, emotions erupting inside me—was my most important asset as a competitor. I could be like that, I believed, because I inherited two contrasting personalities. My father was as low-keyed and complacent as you can get. My mother is an emotional, very high-strung person. My father gave me self-control in time of stress; my mother, the overdrive to succeed whatever the cost.

I think you will find this dual personality in many successful people in any competitive profession. The obvious prerequisite for success in competition is an abundance of talent. But as you rise to higher levels you compete against other people who are equally talented. Then you need intensity, a killer instinct that impels you to keep going the extra mile to reach a goal when others slow down or stop.

On a basketball court I had that instinct. I would climb over anyone or anything to succeed, whatever the cost to me or anyone else. Some years ago I was playing in an ordinary three-on-three half-court game at my basketball camp for boys in New Hampshire. One of the players was a boy from Colgate named Duffy, who worked for me as a counselor at the camp. Everyone liked him—he was a decent, nice young man.

Well, we were banging around under the hoop and he made contact with me. I went wild. I flung an elbow into his face. He fell to the ground but he still had a grip on the ball. As if I hadn't done enough, I went right after him and stole the ball. And while I was jerking the ball away, I kicked him in the face—not intentionally, but not accidentally, either. Blood poured from a cut above his eye.

I didn't even stop playing. Someone else took the kid's place while I went on doing my thing out there, playing better now because of the anger he had aroused.

As soon as the game ended, what I hope is my basic nature came to the fore. I felt terrible. I went to the infirmary and spent about an hour with Duffy, telling him how badly I felt.

Yet I knew I would do the same thing again in the heat of competition. In fact, even during meaningless regular-season games I hoped that someone would knock me down, because I played better when I was angry. I believe that if I had never had this killer instinct, this inner drive to keep going when others slowed down, I would have been just another of those six-foot guards who wander briefly into the NBA and then disappear without a trace.

We won that game against the Lakers for the National Basketball Association championship, the fifth in a row for the Boston Celtics. After that game I retired. I was thirty-five and I could have played for another year or two. But I had always wanted to retire when the Celtics and I were on top.

I was well prepared to leave basketball. I had signed contracts with three companies to do public relations and sales work. I was the partner in an insurance company in Worcester, Massachusetts, where I lived with my wife Missie and our two daughters. I had come to Worcester eighteen years earlier, as a freshman at Holy Cross, and had lived there ever since.

But I didn't want to leave basketball. For one thing, it's only natural to love something you do well. And I had learned from working at my camp that I enjoyed teaching the game to young players. There was more to it than that, though. Looking back, I realize that I was reluctant to give up competition. I had honed my life to a competitive edge, and now, if I couldn't compete myself, I could at least compete through the team I coached.

So when Boston College offered me the position of basketball coach, I thought: *Exactly what I want to do.* The job would keep my hand in the game yet would last only from September to March, leaving me time for my other commitments. And I would be close to home. BC's campus at Chestnut Hill is only an hour's drive from Worcester.

Like many men dedicated to a career, I had been able to give little time to being a family man. From the day I came out of college, I had been wrapped up in my career: traveling with the Celtics during the season, keeping myself prepared physically and mentally, doing all the things that seem to be required of sports celebrities. I had not had the hours to devote to my wife and daughters, who were by this time almost teenagers. Now I thought I could be home with them more often without leaving basketball altogether.

As a coach I had high hopes that the Cousy name would attract the kind of player I wanted—poor and as hungry to succeed as I had been. I grew up in a poor neighborhood on New York's East Side and moved to Queens when I was twelve. There I played schoolyard basketball on the twin principles that you gave it back "in spades" to anybody who gave it to you and that every loose ball was mine.

In my years at BC we tried to develop that kind of player. These young men received a basketball education and a good college education, as well. And in the process I got an education, too.

I experienced the many pressures that most college coaches (and others in competitive businesses) must cope with. The biggest pressure of all was to win games. Though some of the pressure came from others, much of it I put on myself. But there were other conflicting demands—demands that you be honest with your players, that you live within the rules governing college basketball and that you hold on to your own sense of right and wrong. I learned that there were some situations where my killer instinct conflicted with my need to stay honest. And I came to see for the first time that winning might not always mean success and happiness. I had always assumed that winning *was* success.

*Winning at Any Cost* might well be the chapter heading when future historians tell the story of the American society of our time. I came out of the big-city ghetto chasing after the American Dream with millions of young men and women of my generation. The dream was to get rich, be famous, be a success.

Success. Winning. They are words stitched into the national fabric along with the stars and stripes. Growing up during World War II, I remember learning early that America had never lost a war. I saw friends marching off to Korea in the 1950's repeating that line. A dozen years later we were ridiculing any "no-win" policy in Vietnam. The American will to win at any cost prevailed and we would not leave that tortured country until we had sounded a victorious note—"Peace with honor."

Then came Watergate. Again, men of my generation showed they would do anything to succeed. "I'd walk over my grandmother to win an election," Charles Colson said. The operative words were "Do what has to be done, but don't get caught." We had come to a time and place in history where the White House itself offered the oldest of apologies for wrongdoing: the end justifies the means. Reelecting Richard Nixon was good for this country and its people; hence, any means justified that end.

Which one of us hasn't used that same excuse? If I would run over someone in a casual game of basketball, could I blame Charles Colson for being willing to run over his grandmother to win an election? The pressure is always there for most of us. Win or be fired, the coach is told. Sell the product or be gone, the salesman is told. The boss doesn't want excuses, he wants results. "Winning isn't everything," Vince Lombardi told us, coaches and non-coaches, "it's the only thing."

Conversely, if winning is the only thing because it is the American Dream come true, then losing is the American Nightmare. The word *loser* is a dirty word in our society. Call a man a son of a bitch and he may grin; you've made him sound tough and manly. Call him a loser and he may fight you because you've made him sound unmanly. Again sport has given us the operative phrase: "Nice guys finish last."

What I found both curious and frightening about my need to win was that the more I won, the more pressure I felt to keep on winning. You would think that when a man has proven himself to be among the best, there would be no need for him to keep on proving it to himself. Already as a player I had learned that accomplishment increased pressure rather than decreasing it.

During my first few years in the NBA, I thought I was the best basketball player in the world. I thought I could go out there on any given night and do my thing and no one was going to stop me with any consistency. I never worried about failing.

By my last season, I was known as the greatest guard of my era. But I was also slower. I was aware that other people were making it tougher for me to do my thing. At times they could make me look bad.

I told myself, *Why worry? There's money in the bank. I don't have to go out there every night and worry about performing at a child's game.*

Yet I could visualize some father sitting in the stands and saying to his son, "Look, there's Bob Cousy, the greatest player in the world," and there I am tripping over my feet. I worried that people expected me to do certain things that I couldn't do any more.

What I also found, both as a player and as a coach, was that not everyone had my intense desire. I saw many immensely talented players who never seemed to use all of their potential. Jerry Lucas, for instance, could have been one of the half-dozen outstanding forwards of his time. Even by employing only 80 percent of his potential, he was an All-Star for several seasons. But people with less talent could shut off Lucas, nullify him, and Lucas seemed unwilling or unable to get that other 20 percent out of himself to get by those people.

For a long time I couldn't understand people like Lucas. I'm still not sure that I do. But after my ten years as a coach (six years at Boston College and four years in the National Basketball Association), I wonder who has the more cogent approach to competition, the Cousys of the world or the Lucases.

The six years at Boston College were mostly winning, fulfilling years. But one day I sat down and wrote out my resignation, ending what to this day I still consider the happiest six years of my life.

Shortly after I left Boston College I signed to coach the Cincinnati Royals in the NBA. I left Worcester, opening up a new gap between myself and my family. I did it for the same reason many of us do things we don't want to do: for money. Offered $100,000 a year, I couldn't say no.

For the next four years I attempted to turn around what was a mediocre team in the NBA. Although the world of pro basketball was familiar to me, I had to face new kinds of pressure. Now I had to attract paying customers. I had to deal with players who were the pampered products of college recruiting. And now, for the first time, I learned what it was like to be a perennial loser in the league standings. Although winning had magnified the pressures, winning also had its rewards. Losing had none. I was drinking Scotch out of water glasses to make sleep come easier, and all my normal appetites diminished or disappeared. Shortly after the start of my fifth season as a pro coach, I walked away once again—quitting a $100,000-a-year job. These experiences, as a winning coach at Boston College and as a losing coach in the NBA, led me to take a closer look at what I thought were the real priorities of my life. I had always wanted to be a success in anything I tried. In any competition I had an almost uncontrollable need to win. This killer instinct had brought me success as a player and as a coach, but it also tempted me to run over people, to break rules, to neglect my family, to neglect myself to the point where I was on the edge of physical and emotional breakdown. I had always admired the killer instinct but now I had seen what it had done to me and where it had led the people who brought us Vietnam and Watergate.

I had begun to question my attitudes about winning and losing. This book is about ten years in coaching, the questions I began to ask myself, the answers I am still struggling for.

# WINNING

# THE END –
# AND
# THE BEGINNING

During the summer of 1968 I was watching some kids scrimmage at Graylag, my basketball camp in New Hampshire. Suddenly I found myself following a tenacious little guard named Bobby Griffin. He was good. *I didn't realize Bobby had improved so much*, I thought.

Griffin had been coming to my camp since he was a youngster, first as a camper and now as a counselor. I knew his parents and had admired Bobby's devotion to basketball, but I had never seriously thought of him as a recruit for my Boston College team until this moment. I saw that he was reasonably quick, had a good shot and played excellent defense. Though he was not an outstanding prospect—the blue-chipper college coaches dream about—I thought that with some polishing he could probably be a starter for BC as a junior or senior.

I knew that Bobby had received a partial scholarship from Columbia University, but it did not cover his full expenses. Finally I made a proposal to Bobby. I was frank about his prospects with the team yet let him know that I would like to have him come to BC and could offer him a full athletic scholarship.

Bobby was delighted and so were his parents. The new arrangement required the approval of the Columbia coach, Jack Rohan, since Bobby had already officially accepted the scholarship there. Jack may have been reluctant, but he went along. Bobby came up to BC and talked to the admissions staff and the dean of the department he was interested in. He was accepted for admission and I told the Griffins that they would receive the offer of a full scholarship in the mail.

A few days later I got a call from Bill Flynn, BC's athletic director. "About this boy Griffin," he began. "We may have some trouble with the NCAA about this. You know the rule—you can't recruit a boy who attended your camp as a junior."

The NCAA was not my favorite organization. In five years as a coach I had felt restricted before by their picky regulations. At the same time, I had learned that their major rules governing recruiting were largely unenforced. But this time I was sure there had been some mistake. "Hell," I said, "Bobby has been coming to my camp for years and I never even considered recruiting him until this summer."

Bill was skeptical. He was an official of the NCAA and a stickler for the rules. I explained the situation and Bill agreed to request permission from the ECAC (the regional representative of the NCAA). A few days later he called me. The NCAA had answered: Permission denied.

I couldn't believe it. I had given Bobby and his parents my word. It seemed too late for them to make other arrangements. Bill said he was sorry, but there was nothing further he could do.

I hung up the phone and wrote our my resignation, to be effective at the end of the coming season—my sixth at Boston College.

The Griffin incident was not earthshaking in itself. Bobby's family had been put in a difficult position (he eventually enrolled at Columbia). I had been embarrassed by making promises I couldn't keep. The NCAA rule seemed wrong-headed or at least wrongly applied. But I had faced greater disappointments and survived.

Yet for me the Griffin case forced recognition of a conflict that had been building over my five years as a college coach. I had been winning more than my share of games, but that hunger in me to be perfect was tempting me to ignore only NCAA rules but my own sense of right and wrong. It was suddenly clear to me that I couldn't win as much as my hunger called for and still keep from compromising. I didn't know how much of the fault was mine and how much was the "system's," but I knew that I had to walk away from the situation before this conflict destroyed me.

I had come to Boston College five years earlier in the fall of 1963 certain that I would be a successful coach. BC was not a major basketball power. The previous year's team had won ten and lost fifteen—and the sport took a back seat to both football and hockey. The school had no intention of developing a national champion. But I shared the belief of the people who hired me that with my background I could at least put BC basketball on the map of New England.

After thirteen years with the Celtics, I felt that I came with real coaching credentials. At my basketball camp in New Hampshire I thought I had learned the patience required to teach basketball to young players. In my pro career as a playmaker and team captain I had learned the strategy and psychology of the game. And I had played under two master coaches.

The first was Buster Sheary, my coach at Holy Cross during my junior and senior years. I had come to college a hungry athlete and Buster had made me hungrier. If you want to win badly enough, he told us, no one can stop you from winning. Toward the end of practice he would roll a basketball out the door of the gym, which sat on the top of a hill. We would chase after it, and the one who came back with the ball would go to the shower first. More often than not, I got the ball.

Before a game Buster would stand up and wave a flag, goading us or pleading with us to blow the other team off the floor. This cliché described Buster perfectly: When he asked you to run through a wall, your only question was "Which wall?" Buster was no actor. He did not fabricate emotion. He taught me that players at any level—college or pro—will respond to genuine, sincere appeal. Years later, in the supposedly sophisticated seventies, Buster would show me that such an appeal could still be effective.

The other coach was the obvious one. The newspapers call him Red Auerbach, but I always called him Arnold. In terms of teaching X's and O's to players, there were many NBA coaches at least the equal of Arnold. I don't think we used more than six plays in my thirteen years as a Celtic.

Arnold coached with much the same philosophy as the late Vince Lombardi: It's not so much what you do that counts, it's how well you do it; keep it simple and execute properly. It was a lesson I would forget during this first year at BC.

Arnold's other contribution to the Celtics was his ability to keep us motivated year after year. We might have won four championships in a row but he stayed on top of us, letting us know that he had forgotten all about those four straight titles and was now interested only in winning the fifth. More than any one of us, Arnold was responsible for keeping the Celtics number one for so long.

And, of course, I had learned a few things about coaching during my years as captain of the Celtics, developing my own ungentle personality. During time-outs I could be bitchy. I'd say, "Tommy, your guy got the last six, let's shut his ass off." Or: "Goddamnit, Russ, he's hitting over the top, go out on that bastard before we make a hero out of him." I knew my college players would feel the sting of that tongue, too. Nothing short of perfection was good enough, although I knew that a coach, like a playmaker, must also be willing to take the blame when a mistake was his.

So all in all, I thought I had a reasonably good grasp of the basics of coaching: motivation, handling people and a sense for the game learned in twenty years of running up and down basketball courts. But I had more to learn than I expected.

Immediately, I liked the atmosphere at Chestnut Hill. I was being paid $12,000 a season, a little higher than the average at that time for an Eastern college basketball coach, but the money was secondary; I was also earning income from my public relations jobs. What had brought me here was to teach a game that had been my life.

The president of Boston College, the Very Reverend W. Seavey Joyce, and the athletic director, Bill Flynn, made me welcome from the very start. Though Bill wanted to win every bit as badly as his coaches, he refused to compromise the rules. We would have disagreements, but I always respected Bill's position—and would even wonder in later years if Bill hadn't been right most of the time. I had two assistants. Frank Power had been interim basketball coach the year before. He was basically an academician, a good teacher with a sharp analytical mind. In addition to helping me with the varsity, he would be coaching the freshman team. My second assistant, John Magee, was cut from my "ghetto mold." He was young and had a close relationship with the players. Both Frank and John had the drive and intensity I admired and felt was necessary for success.

I had come to Boston College feeling I was entering a relatively low-pressure situation, yet I was anxious, like most beginners, to succeed right away. During those first pre-season practices I had a list of things to teach as long as my arm. I taught a comprehensive course on basketball; as a result, I didn't leave time for practicing the bread-and-butter skills that win basketball games. In short, I over-coached.

When the season started, the team seemed disorganized. I suppose they had learned so much that they didn't know which skill to use first. We lost six of our first eight games. We had better material than the record showed, and I began to see the error of my ways.

And I was beginning to recognize that being a coach was a little different from being captain of the Celtics. Even though the team was not playing well, I began to recognize that I was relying on the players—and on a few talented players in particular. I couldn't score a single point myself.

My best player was a sophomore named John Austin. John was from Washington, D.C., and was the only black player on the team. Arnold Auerbach had told me about him when I was still with the Celtics and I had helped recruit him. I knew already that in his first year with the varsity John would be a star, averaging more than twenty points a game. He was head and shoulders above the others in talent, and generally cooperative, but he knew his importance.

I had resolved to treat all players the same, yet I didn't. During this first season we had a player on the freshman team whose potential was so great that it was generally felt he would be an All-America. I'll call him Robert. He was big, quick and well-coordinated. My mouth watered when I thought of next year's team with both John Austin and Robert. Robert could help put us on the basketball map sooner than we had hoped.

Then one day during the season he came to my office. He wanted to go home. Suddenly I saw my potential All-America going to another team and our next season going down the drain. I talked with him for an hour. His reasons for wanting to leave were vague. He was an eighteen-year-old on his own for the first time, homesick, a little afraid of the academic pressures. I wasn't even sure how determined he was to leave.

But I could take no chances. I called my wife and told

her we would be having a visitor for the weekend. I took Robert to Worcester, fed him steaks, even asked my daughters to help reassure him. I must have been a spectacle—a coach old enough to know better—begging a teenaged player to change his mind.

Finally he agreed to stay, and he came back to BC the next fall. Perhaps because I had been so easy on him the first year, he got into some minor disciplinary trouble that second season. After that, he played for the team, but he never realized the potential I had seen in him.

I hadn't done Robert or myself any favor by getting on my knees. I should have said, "If you want to go home, pack your bags and catch the next plane. But we've lived up to our promises and I think you're making a mistake." I think he would have stayed. His attitude would not have been ruined and I would not have set a bad example by showing the team that I would bow to a show of temperament. In the years to come, I was tempted more than once to beg a player, but I never made that mistake again.

After a shaky start in those first eight games, we did a little better than break even for the rest of the year. There were some disappointments—especially two losses to Holy Cross. The Cross was BC's traditional rival (both schools were run by the Jesuits, who loved to needle each other). It was also my alma mater and was located in my adopted hometown, so I hated like hell to lose.

The last game was against Boston U., and we won it 61–60 on a free throw with three seconds left. Our record was ten wins and eleven losses, an improvement over last season but not good enough for me. I couldn't remember the last time a team of mine had lost more games than it won, and I wasn't about to settle for a string of .500 seasons.

Looking forward to next season, I was already plotting to improve our showing.

# PRESSURES

A few weeks after the season we had a break-up dinner for the team to honor the graduating seniors. I knew I would be speaking and I decided to tell the group where I thought we were going. I was so concerned about doing better that I decided to make some predictions at the banquet, something I had seldom done in all my years in the game.

First, I told them, this had been a disappointing season. We had been slow getting together and we hadn't really played up to our potential. I pointed out that this was the coach's responsibility and that the situation could not be repeated. I went on to predict flatly that as long as I was coach we would never again lose two games in a season to Holy Cross and never again would we lose more games than we won.

I made these predictions to bolster the team's confidence and my own. I knew that a team with a strong belief in itself could sometimes win even when the other team had all the advantages. But perhaps my emphasis on winning games was excessive. I suppose I had been more frustrated by the season than I realized. In a way I was piling pressure on myself to win those games next season. And the message I left with those players probably outdid Vince Lombardi. From all I said, they could only conclude that winning *is* the only thing.

As spring came to the campus on Chestnut Hill, I found myself coming to the office even though the season was over. It was time to recruit, and I was gradually learning what a big part of my job that would be. My expectations that the coaching job would be a six-month-a-year affair began to wither.

Jerry Tarkanian, the coach at the University of Nevada—Las Vegas, has said, "Show me a coach that likes golf and I'll show you a loser." I soon understood what he meant. On spring afternoons when I was scheduled to play golf I would stay at the office until the last minute, making fifteen or twenty calls to line up recruits. Once on the course I would begin to think, *If you had stayed and made the twenty-first call, you might have gotten that blue-chipper.* Even worse was the thought that at the moment I was teeing up, some harder-working coach might be stealing a prospect from under my nose.

Even during the summer I concentrated on BC basketball. Although I still enjoyed my weeks at camp in New Hampshire, the program there had taken on new meaning. Among the counselors were current BC players and recruits who would be entering BC as freshmen. And of course I began to look at every talented basketball camper as a prospect for BC.

When practice began in the fall of 1964, we avoided the mistake of the previous year. We concentrated on basics and on strategies that this team could use to get the most from its talent. On offense we worked on a cohesive fast break and complemented it with a very simple pattern for situations where deliberate play was called for. On defense we worked on an aggressive man-to-man and on special pressing defenses to harass poor ball-handlers on opposing teams. John Austin was back, and we had a fine ball-handler in Ed Hockenbury. A promising sophomore center, Willie Wolters, would help with rebounds.

This season we started out on the right foot. After winning four of our first five games, we went to the Milwaukee Classic Tournament, meeting Wisconsin in the opening round. We played a good, strong game, but with four seconds left we were behind 85–84.

I called time out. In four seconds we had to move the ball across midcourt, pass it to someone in position, and then put it through the hoop or draw a foul. I began to diagram a play, not without some feeling of hopelessness: we had a long way to go and very little time to get there.

John Austin interrupted me. "Hey, Coach," he said, "just give me the ball and I'll put it in the hole."

A coach usually listens when a player asks for the ball in that situation. Too many players want to run away from it when the chips are down. "John," I said, "if you feel that way, the ball is yours."

We passed the ball to him. He dribbled for three seconds near the midcourt line, then let go a long forty-five-foot jump shot. The ball was hanging in the air when the buzzer sounded. Then down it came right through the basket for the two points that won the game.

It was a beautiful shot and a dramatic moment. Ironically, it was decisive for John Austin as well as for the team. He had proved his courage in a tense situation and he had proved once again that the jump shot is the most devastating shot in basketball. But unfortunately he had also proved—at least to his own satisfaction—that his talent exempted him from being a team player. Although he was still our leading man through that season and the next, Austin never again quite fit into our offensive patterns. With his great talent, he did not see the importance of improving other skills during his stay at BC. When he tried out for the pros, he learned that nearly every pro rookie could shoot as well as he could. He had to be able to do other things, and he couldn't do them well enough.

It is because of the jump shot, I was discovering, that many of today's kids don't do other things on the court as well as the kids of twenty years ago. For example, I was finding it very difficult to get my team to play strong sustained defense for an entire game. In basketball, shooting is fun; defense is work, requiring extreme, sustained concentration. One of my players might sustain his defense for a whole game only to discover that his man still scored twenty points instead of his usual twenty-five. *Big deal*, he would say to himself. *All that effort and what difference did it make? A handful of points*. He would be only human if he didn't play defense with less concentration the next time.

Because they shoot so well, many players stand around when someone else on their team has the ball. They don't move without the ball or develop a play because the effort becomes unnecessary, even wasted. Why run through a complex pattern when one pass and a jump shot can get the same two points? They also give little time to such basics of the game as passing and dribbling. And since they spend so much time working on shooting, they don't think the game as well as they should.

After that last-second victory over Wisconsin, we slumped a little. We lost five of our next eight games and our record was now eight wins and six losses. I looked back at my banquet predictions and shuddered a bit.

But then everything fell into place. We beat Rhode Island by two points in the closing minutes, then won our next eight games in a row. Now that we had a 17–6 record, people on Chestnut Hill began to notice basketball. Roberts Center held 3,000 people, and late in that 1964–65 season the sport was filling it for the first time in years. Thanks to the team, my promise of a winning season had come true.

Our next game was in Worcester against Holy Cross. The usual rivalry between the schools was intensified this year because the winner was likely to receive an invitation to the NIT, the big post-season tournament in Madison Square Garden. Like the Wisconsin game earlier, this one went down to the final moments. With seven seconds left, we had the ball and the score was tied. Once again we went to our strength, giving the ball to John Austin. He drew a foul, went to the line and made the shot to win another close one. We had made good on the second part of my banquet promise, and we received our invitation to the NIT.

We won our last four games (including a second win over Holy Cross) and then headed for the Garden, where we lost in the first round to the St. John's team that won the tournament. But the season had been a resounding success. We had a 22–7 record, and John Austin had been named to some All-America teams along with such major college stars as Bill Bradley, Cazzie Russell and Gail Goodrich. BC fans and basketball buffs were astonished at our progress—and I was a little surprised myself.

As I had already learned, my job was not finished when the last game was played. After the season came the last big recruiting push. Austin and Hockenbury had one more season. There would be some good sophomores up from Frank Power's unbeaten freshman team. Next year seemed promising, but what about the year after, with my two big guns graduated? A coach learns to look—and worry—far into the future. I concluded I needed a blue-chipper right now, to play on the freshman team next season and take over for Austin the year after. After a winning season like the one just concluded, I'd better produce more winners in the years to come. The pressure was beginning to build.

Through April and May I spent hours on the phone, talking to BC alumni, prospects and prospects' parents. I visited the homes of those who were most likely to come to BC. And I helped play host when the boys made their forty-eight-hour visit to campus.

Each school was supposed to offer the same package: tuition, room, board and fifteen dollars a month for laundry. Of course, there were rumors everywhere that this maximum offer was being exceeded every day. When I was with the Celtics we tossed the same joke at every All-America player who joined the team: "Hey, kid, you must be taking a pay cut to come to the pros."

There were also ways—technically illegal—to keep students in school once they arrived. When I was a senior at

Holy Cross my father became seriously ill and I informed the authorities that I might have to drop out of school. Suddenly an alumnus offered me the loan of his car so that I could drive down to New York to see my father. Other old grads handed me small amounts of money. The gifts came to only a few hundred dollars altogether, but they had the desired effect: I was able to keep playing and finish out the year.

So I knew what I could offer by the book and a little about how the rules were bent or broken.

Like every salesman, a coach learns to take advantage of the strengths of his product—the school and its basketball program—while playing down its weaknesses. When I talked to prospects I found myself emphasizing the quality of education they could get at BC. This attracted some players, but I found it scared others away: some were so unsure of their academic ability they didn't want to risk going to a "hard" school.

I found that my best recruiting weapon was the promise that a boy would play and not sit on the bench. A lot of talented kids want to go to UCLA or North Carolina State or a Big Ten school—but the coach can play only five at a time. He may have five happy starters and ten very unhappy reserves grumbling about not getting a chance. When I was trying to recruit a talented player, I let him know that he had an excellent chance of starting for me, even as a sophomore (freshmen couldn't play varsity ball at that time).

In my first year of recruiting, I promised a big center, Willie Wolters, that if he would come to BC, I wouldn't recruit another top center. Willie could have gone to a big basketball school, but he might have ended up on the bench. He was smart enough to pick a school where he was sure he would play. Of course, I was taking a gamble. If Willie had developed too slowly, or if he had been hurt, I would have been without a center. But the gamble paid off.

When a prospect visited BC, I talked to him over dinner and had the captain or another player show him the campus and arrange meetings with deans or professors in his particular field of interest. We provided modest entertainment—a hockey game or a movie on Saturday night, as a rule. I learned gradually, however, that my idea of a good time for a high school prospect might be a little out of date.

I had been trying to recruit a quick, high-scoring forward from a town in upstate New York. I had visited the boy's home early in my second season, talked to his parents and gotten a promise that he would accept our scholarship and enroll at BC.

In December or January, however, the boy called me and said he had changed his mind. He was going to one of the big schools in the South. I wished him good luck, hung up and tried to figure out how this could happen. Later that afternoon I was sitting in the cafeteria with Frank Power and John Magee. Some of the players were sitting at a nearby table. I saw one player whose background was similar to that of the boy we lost and I asked him to come over to our table.

"We just lost a prospect who lives close to your hometown," I told him. I mentioned the name of the school the boy had picked and asked, "Why in the world would a kid like this decide to go to a big school so far from home when he could go to BC?"

The player smiled. "Coach, if you had been invited down to that school, you wouldn't be asking me that question. I visited there twice. The first time, as I got off the plane, I was introduced to an old grad who was to become my 'angel' if I stayed. He took me downtown and bought me a wardrobe of clothes. He told me he would give me a specific sum of money every time I had a good game for the varsity. Then he took me out to the coach's home where four or five other recruits were being royally entertained. That night the 'angel' got me a date. And I was told these 'privileges' could be extended for the next four years."

As I sat there listening, I couldn't help but draw comparisons to our own entertaining. But if we were behind the times, so were the NCAA rules. Clothes, girls and performance bonuses were not part of the NCAA code, yet apparently they could be offered and accepted with impunity.

I was beginning to see that when I came to BC I had been a babe in the woods—and not just about NCAA regulations. On one of the first days in my office at Roberts Center, a janitor had said to me, "Ask for whatever you want now, because after you've been here a while, you won't be able to get it." He was talking about furniture, but now—almost two years later—I realized that his advice applied to other things as well.

In talking to other coaches and seeing how they operated, I learned that BC was behind the times in many ways. Some schools admitted junior college transfers; we didn't. Some schools had two or three full-time assistant coaches to go out on the road and recruit; we had two part-time assistants. I didn't think BC should become a basketball factory. But I also didn't like to compete with one hand tied behind my back.

When I had first arrived at BC as a so-called name coach, I could have asked Bill Flynn for a bigger budget, reconsideration of entrance requirements or whatever else I thought I needed to compete on even terms with most schools on our schedule. I would probably have gotten much of what I asked. Trouble was, I didn't know at the time what to ask for.

Now, feeling the pressures of this winning season, I was also handicapped by my success. If I asked for more now, people could ask why I needed more money, staff or anything else when I had just won twenty-two games with existing resources. I had understood the janitor's warning too late.

But I probably wouldn't have asked even if I had known what to ask for. It just isn't my nature. At first I blamed Bill Flynn for not offering changes. However, in fairness, I was the one that should have pushed since basketball was my specific responsibility. If I had asked for changes and fought for my case, I'd probably still be coaching at Boston College. Like most coaches, I'm always second-guessing myself.

# WALKING
# THE EXTRA
# MILE

**W**e played our first game of the 1965–66 season, my third at BC, against Dartmouth. We rode up to Hanover in a bus. Usually on these trips I would read, but during the last hour or so of the ride I had to put the book aside, a pain across my middle making me bend over and grip a railing in front of me.

When we arrived at the Hanover Inn, I had to be helped to a seat in the lobby. The pain was so intense I couldn't straighten up. Some of the players had invited their parents to come up for the game, and they brought them over to me to say hello. I felt like an idiot, mumbling my greetings curled up in the chair like a ball.

Someone suggested I lie down on a bed. After an hour of agony I was convinced that I was sick enough to be taken to the emergency ward of a hospital. By now everyone with our team was concerned. At the hospital the doctors took x-rays and ran other tests. By now I was thinking, *I've caused so much of a commotion, I hope it's something serious, like a mild coronary.*

The doctors came back with the x-rays. I was twisted up on a bed, still holding my middle. "Well, we found the trouble," one of the doctors said to me. "You have gas."

I couldn't believe it. I stared at the doctor, still clutching my belly. "Gas!" I yelped. I couldn't believe gas could cause what felt like the worst pain of my life. "Doctor," I said, "are you kidding me?"

He said he wasn't kidding. And he explained what had happened. An attack of nerves had acted like two hands to grip a segment of my large intestine, shutting off each end. The segment had ballooned. On the x-rays that segment of intestine, filled with gas, looked like a fat knackwurst. The doctors told me to knead my belly with my hands and the pain would subside. It didn't.

I made myself get up and go to the game, bent over and shuffling like an old man. I watched the game doubled up on the bench. We won, 107–84. At the buzzer I started to get up and suddenly I could stand straight for the first time in hours—the pain had vanished. But I could feel rumblings inside me and I ran for my life to the locker room.

I had recurrences of those intestinal pains throughout the season, some of them so bad I had to crawl along the floor to the bathroom. And I knew what was causing them: the pressure to keep on winning.

I had come to BC looking upon college coaching as a no-pressure situation compared to the championship pressure with the Celtics. No one had expected me to work any miracles and produce a lot of wins. But to everyone's surprise we had put together a 22–7 record in only my second season and gone to a post-season tournament. I felt that people were expecting more winning records and more post-season tournaments. Even if others weren't pressing, I was. It would be hard to settle for a lesser record next year.

"You know," I said to John Magee one day, "two years ago twenty wins in a season would have been looked upon around here as a good reason to hold a parade. But after last year if we win twenty games it's going to be considered a disappointment."

I was learning as a coach what I had learned as a player: success only magnifies pressure.

The way to keep on winning, obviously, was to recruit more blue-chippers like John Austin, who would be graduating at the end of the season.

But I was beginning to think that I had gotten Austin with beginner's luck. I was learning how many extra miles you had to walk to land a blue-chipper. And by now I had more insights into what was necessary to get them.

During that third season I was told about a dinner attended by a number of people prominent in basketball. One of the guests was a coach at a college that was nearly always in the top ten. Over cocktails the talk turned to recruiting. The coach said—boasted, really—that he had hired a bright student to take the College Board tests for a blue-chipper whose jumpshot was considerably more accurate than his answers on tests. The bright student turned in a score of something like 1,400 out of a possible 1,600. Someone became suspicious, took a second look and uncovered the deception. The blue-chipper was not admitted to the coach's school.

You may wonder why a coach would boast about such a deception. Perhaps rule-breaking had become so common that it didn't matter. Or maybe he felt that the violation was less wrong if he could acknowledge it in public.

Earlier, during that summer of 1965, I had begun to understand just what was meant when other coaches said they would offer *anything* to get a blue-chipper. I was at my camp for boys. One of the kids, whom I'll call Donald, was an outstanding high school halfback. At least a dozen big-time football schools were chasing him—he was an excellent football prospect *and* an outstanding student, very gung-ho, very idealistic.

One evening I was sitting in my office when the phone rang. The caller asked for Donald, and I sent someone to get him. When he came in, I told him to take the call in an inner office, where he would have privacy. He was on the phone for fifteen or twenty minutes. When he came back out, his face was white. I thought he was going to faint.

"What's the matter?" I asked him.

He told me the caller had been a well-known, highly respected coach, who had offered to provide for his sex life for the next years, spelling out the possibilities in the bluntest terms.

Unfortunately, that kind of an inducement—a pimp's inducement—must have appealed to many of the kids the coach talked to. The offer even gained respectability because of its source: that coach, in his community and in his state, is considered a pillar of society. Donald, however, was turned off completely. He had lost all respect for the coach. He checked the school off his list and went somewhere else.

At the time, I didn't give the incident much thought. *Well, that particular coach is an exception,* I rationalized. *Not too many coaches would go that far to win.*

I had some evidence to think otherwise after an incident at BC during my third season. We had been corresponding with a six-foot-eight forward who was attending a high school in Georgia. Academically, the boy was weak, although he met the eligibility standards of the NCAA and so could play basketball at most schools. However, BC required much higher scholastic standards than the NCAA minimum and this boy didn't meet them. But BC had started a special black studies program to attract ghetto kids who would not normally be eligible but who showed the potential to attain a degree.

A friend of mine, Dave Nelson, who later ran for Congress and is now a superior court judge, was in charge of picking the kids for the program. I called him. "I know the program isn't there for this reason," I told him, "but we're trying to land a kid who could make us a winner all by himself. I'd like you to meet him and delve into his background. If you feel the potential is there, needless to say it would be very helpful to our program."

Dave agreed to meet him. We flew the boy and his father up from Georgia and had a nice dinner in the school cafeteria—together with my two assistants and their wives, my wife and the captain of the team. The boy seemed soft-spoken and reserved; he made a good impression on everyone. After the dinner the captain took him downtown to a movie.

The next morning I called Dave. "What did you think of the boy?"

"I was kind of impressed," Dave said, but I sensed a hesitancy in his voice.

"What's the matter?"

"Well, there's one little problem, Cooz. After you left,

the father took me aside. He asked me if I would take him downtown and get him a girl."

Dave, understandably startled, told the man that the good Jesuits at BC didn't provide that kind of service. The father then told Dave, in very strong terms, that the service had been provided for him at all the other schools he had visited with his son. This was probably an exaggeration, but it was still a little frightening.

The prospect went to play for a school in the Midwest. Whether he went there because that school took care of Daddy, I don't know. But the incident taught me that what I was offering—Boston College and Bob Cousy— might not be as alluring to many of the blue-chippers, black or white, as the promises some other schools were making.

All in all I thought I had a reasonably attractive package to sell—an assurance the prospect would play, a good education and coaching by Cousy. Like any good salesman I was willing to hit the road to sell that package. The zeal of my Depression-era generation gave me an appetite for work, and to get the kids I needed at BC I was willing to do almost anything—including going the extra mile.

I am sitting in the living room of a house in a small New Jersey town, listening to a seventeen-year-old play the organ. It is one o'clock in the morning. I am trying to stay awake, but I am nodding.

Every college coach has stories to tell about looking at a kid's etchings or smiling appreciatively while Mother shows you his baby pictures. You are here because junior is a blue-chipper, and the recruiting game requires that you do or say nothing to discourage his interest in your school or his faith in himself.

Actually, Bobby Dukiet's organ playing would have been delightful under normal circumstances. But to a man accustomed to falling asleep at ten-thirty, one in the morning is not a normal circumstance.

The previous afternoon, a few hours before a BC game, I had received a phone call from a BC alumnus in New Jersey who was a friend of Bobby and his family. Bobby was a solid blue-chipper, a rangy forward who was being pursued by more than a hundred colleges. He was also a good student and a talented, upstanding individual. I had visited Bobby and his parents earlier, and they seemed to be leaning toward BC.

But on the phone that day the alumnus told me, "Get on down here as soon as you can, Cooz. We're in real danger of losing Bobby. An Atlantic Coast Conference school has been talking to him and he seems interested."

That night I sat on the bench through a game that we won only in the closing moments. Then I drove to the Boston airport, where I boarded a plane and flew to Newark. The alumnus met me and we drove to Bobby's house, arriving around midnight, the alumnus having told the Dukiets that I was coming on this moonlight ride. We sat and talked until well past one, and I finally exorcised the spirit of the ACC.

Flying to New Jersey at midnight and listening to that organ represented the extra mile I was willing to walk to land a blue-chipper. But there were some extra miles I would not walk.

.   .   .

I am sitting in the front seat of an automobile parked on a street in a small town in Pennsylvania. Behind the driver's wheel is a BC alumnus. He has brought me here to meet a high school senior who is probably the best player in the state and maybe the best in the Northeast. If I can recruit this kid, I know I will be going with my team to post-season tournaments for three straight years.

"Here he comes now," the alumnus says. The senior is walking out of a gym after finishing practice.

We shake hands. He is a six-foot-six forward. Years later he is going to be very successful in the American Basketball Association.

We get into the car to drive him to his home. He and I chat. "Look, Coach," the boy begins, looking me in the eyes. "I hope you understand that this is only the second interview I've granted while my season is in progress. It's my policy to wait until after the season is over before I see any coaches."

And he goes on to give me some ten minutes along this line—how valuable his time is, how many coaches are clamoring to see him. Perhaps my own ego is up, but I suddenly want no more to do with him. There is no way I can humble myself in front of him and then, when he comes to BC, climb up on my pedestal, crack my whip and scream, "All right, everything's changed, now you're going to have to live by my rules and not by your rules."

We drop the boy off at his house. "Thank you very much," I say, finally getting in a few words. "Good luck, wherever you may go."

And I turn my back on what could have been three winning years. But I knew they could also be three unhappy years for me, spoon-feeding the ego of a spoiled kid. I had always wanted to win and I had always thought I would do almost anything within reason to win. But now I was seeing things that I thought no one should have to do, not even to win.

# SORE LOSER,
# SORE WINNER

Whatever concerns I was beginning to feel about the means I might employ to win, there was no dilution in my need to win. After we had defeated Dartmouth to open our 1965–66 season, and I got over my gas pains, we played Fairfield, a mediocre team, at home. They beat us 100–93. When the game was over, I angrily told a reporter: "We were reading our press clippings and believed them."

I had always been a sore loser and I preferred to have sore losers playing for me. I detested people who could lose and be happy about it, especially if they were the better team and played poorly. The way to accomplish anything worthwhile is to feel deeply about it, to be concerned to the point of breakdown, to bleed if necessary—even when the opponent is an underdog.

I never let my players make the same mistake again. During the week after the Fairfield game and whenever we played a team we figured to beat easily, I used my sharp tongue. I never oversold an opponent, saying, "This team is better than you think." I might get away with that act once or twice, but after we had blown a couple of underdogs off the court, the kids would have laughed if I tried it again.

Instead, when we faced lesser teams, we ran longer, harder practices. Against a stronger opponent, the big-game atmosphere on campus would help get our kids ready. Against the weaker opponent, my testiness and our thorough preparation would get the message across that I was concerned. We wanted to blow out a weak team early, before it could get a lead and build up confidence. The killer instinct is as important and valuable against weak opponents as against strong ones. To avoid all possibility of loss, I told myself, *Break their spirits. Finish them off right at the start.*

Much to my satisfaction, I think I succeeded in getting that lesson across: never again during my career at BC were we upset by an obviously weaker opponent.

We concluded that season, my third at BC, with a 21–4 record. Again we were invited to the NIT in New York. In the opening round we played a Louisville team that had Wes Unseld at center and won in triple overtime. We lost in the second round to Villanova, 86–85. Our overall record, 22–5, was an improvement over last season's 22–7. But now, for the first time, I was facing a season in which I wouldn't have John Austin.

Looking ahead to that fourth season, I could see that our recruiting efforts were paying off. We had two very promising sophomores: an excellent ball-handling guard, Billy Evans, and a six-foot-seven forward-center, Terry Driscoll. Most of the good players came because of our hard work in recruiting. But the Terry Driscoll case illustrates that the other guy's mistakes and a little luck can also play a part.

Two years earlier I had been told about Terry, who was playing for a Boston high school. I went to see him play, but in that game he got into early foul trouble and never really showed much talent. I went home and more or less forgot about him.

At the end of his senior year, he was invited to play in one of the dozens of All-Star games that are played each spring by high school seniors. These events have been called "flesh markets"—and with good reason. The "flesh" is the kids, and college coaches are the merchants who come to sample and bid on the merchandise.

Usually I avoided these games, not caring to hang around outside the locker rooms waiting to catch the boy by his sleeve, begging him to play at my school. I may have been too proud, but I thought this kind of situation was demeaning.

Still, I was also aware of the realities of my profession. I had to get the horses. So I sent one of my assistants to watch the games and report back. If a prospect seemed interested in BC after talking to Frank Power or John Magee, then I would arrange an appointment with him. John Wooden at UCLA always recruited that way. The boy came to Wooden; Wooden didn't go to the boy. I thought this was the way coaches should recruit.

John Magee went to the All-Star game and came back raving about Terry Driscoll, who had been named the game's most valuable player. But Terry had pretty much decided on his college and that college was not BC.

Shortly after the game, Terry's grandmother died. The

coach at the college Terry was planning to attend appeared at the wake. And it seemed to Terry and his parents that the coach was using the occasion to make a recruiting pitch.

It's hard to decide whether the coach's apparent over-eagerness to land Terry is grim or funny. In any case, his indiscretion soured the Driscoll family and suddenly Terry was interested in BC. I talked to Terry and told him about the one game I had seen him play. Obviously, I had been wrong about him. The Driscolls were a close-knit family, and I began to realize that it might be important to Terry that he be close to home so his family could see him play.

Every recruiter, I had learned, looks for the right button to push. The button may be labeled girls, money, a pro career, playing for a coach named Cousy, special courses, whatever. If you find the right button and press it, said the experts, you get the kid. It was a manipulative attitude, hardly a credit to coaches or players, but it often worked.

"Look," I said to Terry. "At BC you'll be near your parents but you can live on campus. And they'll be able to see you play at all our home games and some of the nearby away games."

He accepted our scholarship offer. I'll never know for sure if it was because of my pitch, but I always felt that in this case I had found the right button.

Terry didn't really qualify as a blue-chipper. He came to us with moves as stiff as starched long johns. But he had one great quality: he was coachable. My assistants and I worked with Terry and the other big men for maybe fif-

teen minutes each day before practice, showing them pi-
vot moves, how to get the proper position, how to throw
up left- and right-handed hook shots. After a few minutes
of teaching, Terry could throw that hook shot or duplicate
those moves as though he had been doing them all his life.
He developed into an All-America player and later played
in the NBA.

We were not always as fortunate. We could spend fifteen minutes a day with another player, working on the
same basic moves, and at the end of four years he still
wouldn't have showed much improvement. Some players
absorb coaching like sponges; others never do. I can't explain why this should be. You might think that the slow
learners are not as intelligent as the faster ones, but I had
coachable players who did poorly in the classroom and uncoachable players who got very good grades. It may be
that some boys lack confidence in their coordination and
have a tendency to freeze mentally or physically when
they try to learn new physical moves.

Working with an uncoachable kid was frustrating. But
working with one Terry Driscoll made up for ten of the
others. Coaching, like other kinds of teaching, can be tre-
mendously satisfying. You can pass along something of
your experience and talents and see yourself reflected in
the receptive student.

With Terry our top gun, we won our first eight games
in the 1966–67 season. The wire services ranked us among
the top twenty teams in the nation—with such bigger basketball schools as UCLA, which had Lew Alcindor, and
Houston, which had Elvin Hayes. For Boston College, al-

ways a football- and hockey-oriented school, to be nationally recognized in basketball was akin to the University of Florida becoming a powerhouse in ice hockey.

More important, I began to have a feeling of family about our basketball program. After practice Frank Power, John Magee and I had dinner in the school cafeteria. We talked over every phase of basketball, swapping ideas. Frank later said that he would never forget those little dinners of ours, and neither will I.

My wife and two daughters were actively involved. They attended many home games, and afterwards we would go to the home of Bill Flynn, the athletic director, to have beer and sandwiches with the assistant coaches, their families and other close friends. When we won, which was often now, there was a warm, festive air to these gatherings.

A year earlier Arnold Auerbach had told me he was quitting as the Celtic coach and he asked if I would be interested in the job. The opportunity was attractive—the chance to go back and coach my old team for a salary three or four times greater. But I said no thanks. Despite the stomach pains and pressures, I was just too happy at BC to want to do anything else.

To me, success in basketball—and in life, for that matter—had always been predicated on a philosophy of attack. Be aggressive. Break your opponent's spirit.

Now I was noticing that many coaches took a more conservative approach. For instance, a team would turn up a few quick hoops in a row and take an eight- or ten-point lead with three minutes left in the game. The coach calls a

time-out and tells his team to bring the ball up slowly, kill
as much time as possible and take only sure shots.

He is following "the book." But what happens next, too
often, is that the team loses its momentum. The players
become overcautious. Even when they do get a good shot,
they're worried about missing—and they do miss.

As a result, the losing team takes the initiative and re-
duces the lead. The team that's ahead gets more apprehensive, makes more mistakes and falls behind. Generally, the
team that can take and keep the initiative in the last moments of a close game is the winner.

In that same situation, I told my players to bring the
ball down-court quickly, not slowly. "Attack," I told them.
"The other team is desperate; they'll be looking to steal
the ball. Look for the one quick shot before the defenses
set. This is our chance to kill them off with lay-ups and
short jumpers."

If the quick shot wasn't there, I told them they should
slow up and force the defense to come out for the ball. But
they should be watching for the chance to attack, to make
that easy basket that would wrap up the game and demor-
alize the opponents.

I began to suspect that the big reason coaches played so
cautiously was to protect their jobs. Under the win-or-
be-fired pressures of the coaching profession, they didn't
feel free to take risks. If a coach follows the book and loses,
he can always say, "I went with the percentages. I did
what everyone has been doing since the Year One in that
situation." If he goes against the book and loses, he is at the
mercy of all the second-guessers, including those who
want him fired.

This is especially true in high-pressure situations. The coach knows that perhaps millions are watching and second-guessing, so he protects himself. In tournament play, for instance, I have seen coaches stall for an entire game, holding the ball and keeping to a minimum the number of shots taken by each side. They weren't any more likely to win this way than by playing their normal offense, but they would lose by fewer points in a low-scoring game. To me this is like standing up in front of your players and saying, "We're beat before we start." But I understood that a ten-point loss would be easier to explain than a twenty- or thirty-point loss.

Even a coach who has made it all the way to the Super Bowl has to look over his shoulder at the wolves. This explains why so many Super Bowl games have been dull. When did you last see a Super Bowl team go for a first down on fourth and a yard? A coach might have a play in his bag that's worked a half-dozen times during the season in this situation—with the same personnel he now has on the field. But damned if he's going to use it here, with maybe half the country watching. He disregards his experience, goes by the book, and punts. He's looking out for his job.

I am not advocating that coaches throw the book away. It makes sense to know what has been successful a high percentage of times in various situations. But it has always seemed to me that the good coach should use his knowledge of his personnel and his instinct along with the percentages. After all, it's the surprise play or the gamble that often wins the game.

Years ago I played a lot of golf with Ken Venturi. He was sometimes critical of Arnold Palmer's aggressive approach to the game. "Nobody can gamble as much as Palmer does," Ken would tell me. "It's going to backfire on the guy."

Taking risks never did backfire on Palmer; his success was built on his ability to "charge," taking chances and making them pay off. When one has the ability of a Palmer, what's the sense of playing conservatively and reaching the green in three shots when you could execute a shot that would put you on the green in two?

I noticed that Venturi seldom three-putted a green. Yet he rarely sank the long putt. He followed the book and aimed for that three-foot circle around the hole. That going-by-the-book approach minimized the number of three-putt greens for Venturi, but I always thought if you have the ability of a Venturi to knock in the long putt, why not go for the hole? A few one-putt holes can win the tournament.

The player or coach who is working with superior talent should be willing to take some risks. Those with ordinary talent should follow the book and minimize errors. In short, keep mediocre talent on a tight rein; unleash superior talent and let it run.

The tactics of the game are something every good coach should have under control, and tactical decisions should be cool and calculating. But my own personality never let me forget for long that there is also a more emotional side to competition.

It is early in the 1966–67 season. Once again, I am sitting in a locked hotel room. I ignore the telephone when it rings. On a tray in front of me are the ruins of a half-eaten lunch. Instead of Frank Selvy and the Lakers, I am thinking about the University of Tennessee basketball team, which my Boston College team will be playing tonight.

After winning eight straight games, we had come here to New Orleans for the Sugar Bowl Classic. We lost our first contest to Utah, 90–88. Now we face Tennessee in the consolation round. I fear my players will not be up for the game since they have no chance to win the tournament. Yet the thought of back-to-back losses on our record at this stage of the season drives me wild. I keep telling myself, *We've got to leave here nine and one.*

Late in the afternoon I leave the hotel room to attend a team meeting. Using a huge stand-up blackboard, I review assignments one last time. I go over each man's individual responsibilities and then I begin to talk about how much this game could mean to us. My throat tightens. I try to force out the words. I can't. I break down and begin to weep.

The players are staring at me. Frustrated because I can't speak, I walk over to that huge stand-up blackboard and punch it with all my strength. It feels like I have broken all the knuckles in my right hand. Someone says the meeting is over, and the players file silently out of the room. I stand there holding my aching right hand, sobbing.

I go back to my room and try to compose myself. I think, *My Lord, I hope I didn't make an ass out of myself.*

There is a knock at the door. I open the door. Standing there is my big captain, Willie Wolters.

"Hey, look, Coach," Willie says. "We had no idea this game meant so much to you. Hell, we'll win it."

And we do, upsetting Tennessee, 68–61. We leave New Orleans nine and one.

· · ·

We finished that season with a 21–2 record and were ranked ninth in the nation. For the third year in a row we were invited to a post-season tournament—this time to the NCAA, which decides the national collegiate championship.

After defeating Connecticut, we traveled to College Park, Maryland, for the Eastern finals. We opened against St. John's, did not play well at all, but won from the free-throw line, putting in thirty-one out of thirty-six free throws.

"I'd like to apologize," I said to the writers in the dressing room. "We have played much better. Tonight we played lousy." I was every bit as unhappy as I sounded.

The next night we played the University of North Carolina. If we won this game we would go to the NCAA finals as one of the top four teams in the country, representing the East against UCLA from the West, Houston from the Southwest and Dayton from the Midwest.

We came out running against a bigger, faster North Carolina team and played very well, executing our fast breaks and patterns as smoothly as we had in any game all year. But North Carolina was controlling the boards, as we had expected, and also outrunning us. At one point they led by fifteen. Late in the third period we narrowed the gap to five, trailing 69–64. But they put in three successive hoops and pulled away to win, 96–80.

North Carolina went to the NCAA finals (UCLA won the championship). We went back to Boston with a 23–3 record for the season and with a coach who was reasonably satisfied. For BC to go so far was an accomplishment we could all be proud of. The team had played opponents well above its class and survived all the way to the quarterfinals of the championship tournament.

On the way home it struck me that I had been happier after losing to North Carolina, but playing well, than I had been after winning against St. John's but playing poorly. As a player I had felt the same way. The joy of winning was always diluted if we had played badly. Now, as a coach, I had an even bigger stake. I felt that the team and its performance were an extension of me. Like the sculptor or the composer, I wanted to be proud of my work of art. I wanted it to be perfect. Perhaps I am elevating coaching to a plane higher than it deserves, but the emotions are the same. If my team looked bad, I felt personally responsible. My unhappiness was simply a manifestation of my own search for perfection.

I had always been a sore loser. Now I realized that for similar reasons I could also be a sore winner. It was not just the score that counted, it was the quality of the performance.

# THE GAMBLERS
# AND ME

During the late summer of 1967, shortly before the start of my fifth season at BC, I was at my camp in Graylag when I got a phone call from New York.

"This is Sandy Smith of *Life* magazine," the caller told me. "We're doing a story on basketball and I'd like to talk to you about it."

"Fine," I told him. "Come on up at your convenience. I'll be here until around the first of September."

A day or so later Smith appeared. I introduced him to my family. We sat down in our home and talked. He said that he wasn't here to talk about basketball after all. He was doing an investigation on gambling.

I should have put up my hand and said goodbye right then. Gambling on basketball games had been a cross on the back of the sport since the point-shaving scandals of the 1950's. At the time, there were rumors that I had been saved from a grand jury indictment only by the intercession of Boston's Cardinal Cushing. At the same time, there was a rumor in New York that a St. John's star had been rescued from a pursuing grand jury only by the intercession of New York's Cardinal Spellman. If the rumors had been true, they would certainly prove that the cardinals were loyal basketball fans. But knowing that they weren't true, I never felt that I had been affected in any way by the scandals of the fifties. I had always been candid in talking about them and about the subject of gambling on sports in general.

Smith questioned me for about an hour. I answered all his questions. I noticed he took no notes nor did he use a tape recorder. But I made no comment and wished him well on his story when he left.

Like all players and coaches, I had had conversations with friends that went this way:

"Bob, I've got a six-pack bet riding on the game tomorrow night. How do you think it will go?"

"Hey, Babe," I'd answer, "we've got a pretty fair team but so do they. If you want to bet, it's your funeral."

We'd laugh and that was that. I could hardly be surprised that friends bet on games; nearly everyone bets, even if it's only fifty cents thrown into the office pool on the World Series. And I could hardly be surprised when friends wanted so-called "inside information" on who was going to win. As God gave some dogs the instinct to sniff for game, he gave gamblers the instinct to sniff for inside information.

What a lot of fans don't realize is that athletes and coaches are not that capable of picking winners. They're simply too close to the situation. I remember one season when Arnold and I sat down and tried to pick the winners of each game on the NBA schedule. We were wrong more often than not; if we had been betting, we would have lost a small fortune. Most players and coaches, I suspect, are so engrossed in the functioning of their own teams that they can't handicap the performances of other teams with any reasonable level of accuracy.

In the old days of the NBA, we'd play in Baltimore or Philadelphia on a Saturday night, then jump on the twelve o'clock sleeper, stay up half the night drinking beer and playing cards, get about three hours' sleep and roll into Boston about seven or eight on a Sunday morning.

Ed Macauley, I and some of the other Catholic guys would attend an early-morning Mass. Then we'd stumble back to a little hotel, the Copley Square, where we would get a few hours of sleep before going to the Boston Garden for the game that afternoon.

Invariably, when we came into that lobby, we'd see half a dozen guys sitting in the corners or behind posts, trying to look nonchalant while they eyed us up and down as if we were race horses going to the post. We knew they were gamblers looking to see what kind of shape we were in for the game.

Sometimes we decided to give them what they were looking for. I'd limp in with my arm under my jacket. Ed Macauley would come in stooped, holding his back. Even before we had finished our Bataan Death March to the elevators, the gamblers were running to put down bets against the Celtics.

They thought they had the edge that every gambler looks for. We weren't hurt, of course. But even if we had been hurt, they could have been wrong betting against us. From what I have seen in hundreds of basketball games, even when a team has to play without its top gun it may still have the advantage.

Let's assume his team has to play without Abdul-Jabbar. The team's back-up center may be getting the opportunity to play a full game for the first time in years. He is going to come out there watering at the mouth to prove that he could be a number one center somewhere else. For years his teammates have had to listen to people say how great Jabbar is. They are human, each with his own ego to feed. They will go out there with fire in their eyes to prove that they have the talent, individually and collectively, to win without Jabbar.

Now look at the opposing team. Their center is sitting in a hotel room and thinking, *Thank God the big guy is hurt while we're here. This is the first time I've been in this town in four years that I could relax the night before a game. I can go out and have a few beers.*

His teammates join him for those beers, telling each other: "Isn't it going to be nice not to have to worry about the big guy?"

Out roars Jabbar's team to play a relaxed opponent. I've seen it happen over and over again: the fired-up team, even without its top gun, wins.

If his team has to play a second game without Jabbar, they may be in trouble. Their back-up center and the rest of the team will probably let down, while the opponent has been stung into playing harder.

But the point is that if you had been the only outsider in the world who knew Jabbar was not going to play in that first game, you would have bet against Milwaukee and you would have lost.

So I never believed that so-called inside information was very valuable. As a player and coach I talked openly with reporters about injuries and about almost anything else. I had the reputation for being friendly and reasonably candid. They presented me to the public as a smart, hustling, winning player and coach. It was a reputation I had worked hard to achieve and maintain for almost twenty years. Then in one day's time I thought it had been destroyed.

A month after Sandy Smith's visit, *Life* hit the stands with his story about how "the mob" had infiltrated sports. The article alleged that Bob Cousy had been involved with known gamblers. Within hours after the magazine appeared, you couldn't find a copy in New England.

I was vacationing in Hershey, Pennsylvania, when I got a call from Sam Cohen, a good friend who was sports editor of the Boston *Record-American.* He gave me the gist of the article and I ran out to buy the magazine. Smith claimed that my name had been found in the notebook of a gambler somewhere. Next to my name was the notation "Skiball," which the article claimed was the nickname of Francesco Scibelli, an alleged gambler from Springfield, Massachusetts, and according to Smith, a friend of mine. Another of my friends, Smith wrote, was Andy Pradella, also of Springfield and identified as Scibelli's partner in bookmaking. The article continued:

> Because they always have such excellent information, the Scibelli-Pradella ring is known as the Scholar Group. Cousy admitted he knew the two were gamblers and that he often talked to them about pro and college teams and their chances of winning.

Smith "quoted" me about my relationship with Pradella and Scibelli:

> "I'd be having dinner with Pradella when Scibelli would come over," said Cousy. "They got together each night to balance the books or something."
>
> Did Cousy realize his friends were using what he told them to fix betting lines and to make smart bets of their own?
>
> "No," said Cousy. "I thought they figured the betting line with mathematics. But it doesn't surprise me. I'm pretty cynical. I think most people who approach me want to use me in some way."

As I continued reading the article, each paragraph was like a body blow to the heart.

> Pradella, he [Cousy] said, invited him to a banquet in Hartford that turned out to be a gangster conclave. "Police were watching the place," said Cousy, "and the whole mob was there."
>
> Cousy defends his actions. "In this hypocritical world we live in," he said, "I don't see why I should stop seeing my friends just because they are gamblers. How can I tell Andy when he calls and asks about a team that I won't talk to him about that?"

After putting down the article, I saw a reputation I had built over twenty years suddenly smashed. Friends advised me to ignore it. "*Life*'s in trouble and just wants to sell copies," they said.

I couldn't ignore it. I drove back to Boston and called a press conference. I stood up in front of some fifty reporters and a battery of television cameras. I was nervous and almost choking with emotion and several times during the conference I broke down. But I made these points:

There was a flock of misquotations, inaccuracies and outright lies in the *Life* article. For example, the so-called "gangster conclave" was nothing more sinister than a sports banquet, and I never told Smith that the mob was there and the police were watching. Scibelli was an acquaintance, not a friend, and Smith had lied when he wrote that I had told him Scibelli was a friend. I had met Scibelli, through Pradella, perhaps eight times in twelve years—hardly the sign of a close relationship, never mind a friendship.

Andy Pradella was indeed a friend of mine, and still is. I had known him for twelve years. I had met him when he sent his sons to my camp. We played golf together a few times a year and often sat down for dinner together after a round. I knew Andy gambled, as do most of us. Yet he was my friend not because he gambled, but because he was and is a hell of a guy.

As for giving Andy inside information, I told the reporters that if Andy ever asked me how the Celtics or BC looked, I would tell him the same things I would tell a reporter who called: "So-and-so is looking good." "We have to polish our defense." Things like that. In other words, whatever I told Andy I would have told anyone else, including the public.

I told the reporters that I felt boxed in: "From my point of view, I think frankly the worst part about this is that I'm not accused of anything and I really can't defend myself. The only thing it seems I've done is establish a continual friendship with a man who gambles."

For the first time in my life, I thought I couldn't hit back myself at someone who had hurt me. But I went to my friends in the media, counting on my candor with them in the past and asking them for their assistance. I phoned friends at the Worcester *Telegram,* Al Hirshberg in Boston, Frank Gifford, Arthur Daley and Milton Gross in New York, Jim Murray in Los Angeles.

"I have done nothing except know a man who gambles," I told them. I knew that I was asking these people to go out on a limb: if something damaging about me came out subsequently, they would look bad. "Without equivocation," I told each of them, "you have my word that this will not backfire on you." Nearly all of them came to my defense with articles, columns or broadcasts.

Now *Life* was on the defensive. One of its representatives replied, "All we said was that Cousy knew a gambler and he admits to that." In an editorial the magazine ducked the central issue—whether I had done anything wrong—and tried another tack: "The fact that one individual was unwise in his friendship for known gamblers is far less important than the depths to which The Mob is infiltrating spectator sports in America and how much it is using players for its own illegal profit."

*Friendship for known gamblers . . . The Mob . . . using players for illegal profit.*

By association, through Bob Cousy's friendship with "known gamblers," *Life* had tied him to "the mob." And the magazine was suggesting that it's all right to destroy the reputation of one innocent individual, "unwise in his friendship," if his "involvement" can help put the spotlight on "the mob."

The end justifies the means. It is a philosophy I had always thought wrong, ever since my days as a student with the Jesuits at Holy Cross.

·   ·   ·

One of the media people who called me after the *Life* article appeared was Howard Cosell. I had known Howard ever since I had been a young Celtic. When we came to play in New York, we would just be settling into our hotel near the old Madison Square Garden when someone would knock at our door. Outside, carrying a tape recorder, would be Howard.

"How about doing a couple of minutes with me?" he'd ask me or my roommate, Bill Sharman. In those days Howard was no celebrity. He had a daily sports show on an independent radio station in New York. By now, in 1967, Howard was nationally known, appearing almost every week on ABC's *Wide World of Sports*. He asked me to appear on Wide World the following Sunday with Sandy Smith. On the show Howard would ask each of us for our side of the story.

I wanted to say yes and catch the next plane to New York to do the show. I was stopped by my lawyer, Richard Crotty. He reminded me that I'd have trouble controlling myself when I met Smith. I had broken down during the press conference, and I knew that if I came face to face with Sandy Smith I'd want to do something drastic. I finally turned down Howard's invitation, but he did appear with Smith alone.

Howard mentioned to Smith the banquet I had attended in Hartford which Smith had called a "gangster conclave." It had been a dinner for a retired fighter who had been active in youth work in Hartford. I had sat at the head table with two well-known "gangsters": Willie Pep and the late Rocky Marciano.

"I know all about that conclave," Howard said. "I was

invited to it. I was supposed to be there as master of cere-
monies, but at the last minute I got an out-of-town assign-
ment. If I had gone to that dinner—or 'gangster conclave,'
as you called it—would that have made me a gangster?"

Howard, you always told it as it was. After that show,
my heart felt light for the first time since the story broke.

That was the end of the *Life* affair. I came out of it
much more acutely aware of the dilemma of anyone in
public life. I had seen politicians and newspapers drag
names through the mud for their own gain. Now I learned
myself how devastating the experience can be. Vindictive
as it sounds, I was happy when *Life* folded. I even imag-
ined that my little fight with them had something to do
with their decline. And I still hope that I meet up with
Sandy Smith one more time before I die.

But I became more discreet. I showed a little less of myself to the public by being more careful answering the
questions of reporters, especially those I did not know.
The whole bad-tasting episode made me begin to realize
how our cynical times have made us afraid of personal
candor: don't say *anything* meaningful and you can't get
hurt, whether you're talking to the media, your boss, your
friends, your family, anyone.

Soon I went back to thinking about basketball. For this
1967–68 season I had Terry Driscoll returning as my top
gun. Terry, now a junior, was showing All-America
promise. But Bobby Dukiet, my blue-chipper, injured
himself and would not play this season nor much of the
next two seasons. With Bobby hurt, I felt even more pres-

sure to go out and recruit to get the horses that would get the W's.

I was learning my way around the recruiting game. The NCAA had dozens of rules covering every aspect of recruiting, and Bill Flynn was adamant that we live up to them. But like other coaches I looked first for loopholes to take advantage of. One rule forbids coaches with camps to invite high school juniors they plan to recruit. I got around the rule by putting promising youngsters on the camp staff as counselors. This complied with the letter of the law but probably violated its spirit.

I was crossing into other gray areas. When we got kids jobs during the school year, NCAA regulations required that their income be paid back to the school to offset the cost of their scholarships. I never asked the kids for the money.

Another rule I evaded was the one against subscribing to scouting reports published by people who scout high school talent all year and make a living by selling their information. Since the rule prohibited coaches from availing themselves of these reports, I asked a priest at BC to subscribe and pass the copies to me.

One of the best of these free-lance scouts is Howie Garfinkel of New York. The Garfinkel report tells a coach everything, including things he might have been afraid to ask: a player's strengths and weaknesses, his age, religion, nationality, race, even the status of his love life. Some kids may agree to enroll at your school, I was learning, if you promise to accept a girlfriend.

Garfinkel was seldom wrong about a boy, and he really told all:

> Top offensive guard in area but lackadaisical attitude toward defense takes him down a notch and some question coachability. . . .
>
> . . . high moral character and inordinate strength (lifts weights for breakfast) . . .
>
> . . . stable team leader and loaded with character and class. . . . Prefers [medical school] . . . . Tenth of 150 [in his class] . . . .
>
> . . . one of nation's best leapers who says hello to God 3 times a quarter . . . .

The Garfinkel report was especially valuable to a smaller school like BC. It could save us the time and expense of an assistant coach's making a two-day trip during which he might not glean as much information as Garfinkel gave us in ten seconds. And Garfinkel told us where he thought the boy was likely to play: Big Time, Upper Major, Middle Major, Top Small College or Small College. If he rated a prospect Big Time, I would not usually try to recruit the boy unless he showed interest in us. With the big schools pursuing him, I would have been wasting time. I never did discover why the NCAA had that rule against scouting reports. After I left BC it was rescinded.

I justified evading this rule—and others—by telling myself that other schools were doing a lot worse. A year earlier an incident concerning a top prospect at a university in the Northeast made me even more aware that some of us were recruiting at a disadvantage.

The player, now a successful pro, was a great leaper and a fine all-round prospect. But when he was a high school senior, we at BC were told that his grade average was under 1.6. This meant, according to NCAA rules, that he could be admitted to a college but wasn't supposed to play intercollegiate sports until his average rose above 1.6. Still, he entered a university known for its interest in good basketball.

One afternoon we were talking about the player in Bill Flynn's office. Someone said that he was supposed to play his first game that night for the freshman team, and we were speculating on how many points he would score.

Bill said something like, "Oh, no, he can't play. His grades are under one-point-six."

We glanced at one another. From everything we had heard the boy was going to play. That night he did play. A few days later I received a newspaper clipping of the game. He had scored something like forty-nine points.

I brought the clipping to Bill's office and showed it to him. "Well," he said, as he looked at the box score, "That college can't do that."

But they were doing it, I told Bill. And so were other schools. We may have been crossing into some gray areas by bending a minor rule here and there, but we were following the basic NCAA rules on recruiting. I believed that other schools were not. So when we went after these kids we seemed to be starting off with one hand tied behind our back.

Whenever the subject of recruiting violations came up, Bill would point out our record. "You've had three successive winning years," he would say. "You've gone to three straight post-season tournaments. What more proof do you want that you can play by the rules and still win?"

But I kept complaining. I was all for playing by the rules. But I thought that everyone on our schedule should be playing by the same rules.

· · ·

The season got off to a rocky start—at least for a team that was coming off a 23–3 season. We were never in danger of losing more games than we won, but we did lose some big games. Two-thirds of the way through the year, we had won eleven and lost seven.

We won our last six games in a row, and despite our record we were invited to the NCAA tournament for the second consecutive year. This time we drew St. Bonaventure—and their six-foot-eleven center, Bob Lanier—in the first round. Lanier controlled the boards at both ends of the court and we lost 102–93.

I couldn't call our season disappointing, not when we had been picked by the NCAA as the best team in New England. But our 17–8 record did not look as imposing as those three twenty-victory seasons that preceded. Now I had Terry Driscoll for one more year and then I would be up against the blue-chip problem all over again.

The 17–8 record wasn't good enough to satisfy me. I was still looking for perfection. But I knew that to attain more of those twenty-win seasons I was going to have to do more things I didn't want to do. I was going to cross over into more of those gray areas, and I knew what came after the gray.

# WALKING
# AWAY FROM
# CHESTNUT HILL

Late in the summer of 1968 I sat down and wrote out my resignation as coach at Boston College, to be effective at the end of the coming season.

I was walking away for what may have seemed to be a trivial reason. As I mentioned earlier, a boy named Bobby Griffin had been coming to my camp since he was eight or nine years old. I had never considered him a recruit for BC—even during the previous summer when he was seventeen and good enough to interest the coach at Columbia, who had offered him a partial scholarship. But in the summer of 1968, I noticed such improvement in Bobby's play that I promised him a full scholarship to BC instead.

Then the NCAA denied us permission to give Bobby the scholarship. I couldn't believe it. The NCAA rule states that a coach cannot recruit a boy who had attended the coach's camp between his junior and senior years in high school. The intention of the rule was to take away from coaches who have camps any special advantage in recruiting boys before they become seniors. But like all rules, it seemed to me, it had to be enforced with common sense. I hadn't tried to recruit Bobby when he was a junior. He was a regular camper who had been coming since he was eight years old.

What made the incident so frustrating was my belief that the NCAA was not enforcing its other rules with nearly that degree of narrowness. While we were being denied Bobby on a technicality, the NCAA seemed to look the other way when a coach hired a stand-in to take a blue-chipper's entrance exam. The coach even felt free to boast about his deed in public. And academic standards for athletes were being evaded.

I also found it hard to swallow the NCAA's hypocrisy. Athletic scholarships were to be called "grants-in-aid" and were supposedly awarded solely on the basis of academic qualifications and financial need. Athletic ability was incidental. Naturally, this is pure garbage and the whole world knows it. Yet coaches and athletic directors were expected to give the public this line with a straight face.

No doubt the men at the NCAA were honorable. But when it came to questions of academic standards and recruiting violations, they buried their heads in the sand. As the accounts of violations filled newspaper stories, magazine articles and books, the NCAA seemed to feel that if they ignored the situation it might go away. It won't, of course. Things will only get worse until someone establishes and enforces a sensible set of rules.

I couldn't blame Bill Flynn for checking with the NCAA. Our technical violation might as easily have drawn a suspension as some of the grosser violations. Besides, Bill was determined to play by the rules and I respected him for it.

Still, the Griffin incident was only the straw that broke the camel's back and made me resign. The pressure had been building for some time. I hadn't been able to satisfy my own need for perfection. And the temptation to bend and break rules in order to win was growing. Somehow the senselessness of not being able to take Bobby Griffin crystallized my thinking. Either I had to learn to consciously and willfully break the rules or I had to decide to live by them (even the ones that seemed unfair) and get used to playing at a disadvantage and losing my share of games.

The first alternative seemed impossible. Even if Bill Flynn had not been there to watch the rules, I could not have become an amoral big-time recruiter. But the second alternative—subduing my own deep desire to win every game—also seemed impossible. So I decided to withdraw from the conflicting pressures and resign.

Although my first concern was the effect the pressures of college coaching were having on me, I also began to worry about the effect they must be having on the young men we were recruiting. During the previous season we had tried to recruit a blue-chip prospect from upstate New York whom I will call Rojinsky. I hired him as an assistant counselor at camp and talked to him several times, trying to get him to consider BC, but finally he said no.

A couple of months later I received a call from an excited BC alumnus. "You won't believe this, Cooz," he said, "but I just talked to Rojinsky. He said he's interested in

BC again. He took an application from me and he said he's going to send it in.'"

As soon as I put down the telephone, I told Frank Power to start checking the applications coming into the admissions office. We looked for Rojinsky's every day for two weeks—that's how anxious we were. And one day Frank came into my office smiling. "It's in, Bob," he said, "we got the application from Rojinsky."

I dictated a letter to Rojinsky right away, acknowledging receipt of the application and saying that we would get in touch as soon as it was processed.

Frank was staring at a piece of paper on which he had jotted down Rojinsky's name and address. "Hey, Bob," he said, "do you remember his first name?"

"We called him Tim at camp," I answered.

"It says here that his name is William."

We laughed at our suspicions. After all, how many kids named Rojinsky could there be from one small town in up-state New York who were high school seniors and wanted to come to Boston College? But we decided to check with the high school before we sent out a letter guaranteeing him the grant-in-aid.

We discovered that the Rojinsky who sent in the letter of application was not the basketball-playing Rojinsky. The basketball player had given the application to a cousin, a Rojinsky who was something like five-foot-three.

The basketball player had suspected that we would be so ecstastic at getting the application, we would not notice the different first name. And he had come close to being correct. If I had sent out the official scholarship offer, Rojinsky's cousin would have received a free four-year education at BC worth $20,000. We couldn't throw him out of school simply because he couldn't play basketball. A grant-in-aid is supposed to be dependent only on academic qualifications and financial need and cannot be rescinded. I could see myself sitting on the steps of Roberts Center waiting for my six-foot-six Rojinsky when a five-foot-three freshman walks up and says, "Hi, Coach, my name is Rojinsky."

The blue-chip Rojinsky went to another school. He was suspended from the team once or twice for disciplinary reasons and may have been basically a bad character. But I began to wonder. Had we college coaches, who were willing to break or bend rules to recruit Rojinsky, taught him that it was all right not to play by the rules? In Rojinsky's eyes, coaches were successful, respected leaders in our society. From their example, Rojinsky and any impressionable young person could conclude that the way to be a success is to break the rules. *Coach did it, why not me?*

A few of these Rojinskys would go on from college to become professional athletes, even superstars. We put these superstars on pedestals, and our kids emulate them. What would the Rojinskys of the world tell kids about how to be a success in life?

We had one player at BC who heard what some kids were being offered to go to other schools. I believe he began to regret that he had come to a school where he was getting nothing more than tuition, room, board and fifteen dollars a month.

He decided to get a little more. He went to alumni, the kind who jam the dressing room after a game to slap the players on the back and tell them how great they are. He told the alumni some hard-luck stories about relatives being sick at home.

He got fifty dollars here, twenty dollars there. I heard what was going on, but I couldn't prove anything. Did I want to prove something—and risk losing the player? Of course not. I ignored the rumors I heard and avoided the problem.

I was stepping into gray area after gray area. Most of us, in whatever jobs we have, face moral dilemmas from time to time. We ignore wrongdoing that we're in a position to expose and are tempted to do things that are distasteful, dishonest or even illegal. Sometimes we know that if we don't do these things, the boss will get someone who will.

Taking the high road and resigning from college coaching was easier for me than for most others. I had money in the bank and other sources of income. Still, I was leaving something I had enjoyed very much. It was hard to live with the pressures of coaching, but I knew that with my competitive nature it would be hard for me to live without them.

My resignation was announced on January 20, 1969. At that point the team had won ten and lost three. From there on, we won every game, stretching our winning streak to sixteen games, still a BC record and at the time the longest unbeaten string of any major college team in the country. We finished with a 21–3 record and were invited to the NIT at Madison Square Garden.

This would be our third NIT. In our two previous appearances we had lost in the first and second rounds. We drew the University of Kansas as our first opponent.

Kansas came into the Garden with a forward line as imposing as the Berlin Wall. Their center was six-foot-ten, their forwards six-nine and six-six. Under the boards they would tower over our biggest man, six-foot-seven Terry Driscoll.

But Terry, who was the nation's third leading rebounder, managed to get his share of rebounds and we were able to use our speed against the slower Kansas team. With twelve minutes left we led, 58–44. But then Driscoll committed his fourth foul.

Terry was a smart player and I decided to leave him in the game, hoping he could avoid committing another foul, which would put him out of the game. Against the three Kansas giants, however, he couldn't avoid the foul. With almost a full quarter left, we lost our only effective rebounder.

I told my players to begin our stall, trying to force Kansas to come out to get the ball. Kansas refused, hanging in a zone defense around the basket. Our two ball-handlers, Evans and O'Brien, started to dribble the time away for as long as two minutes at a stretch, and the critical New York crowd began to boo.

Without Driscoll, I decided I had to play this way. "As long as we're ahead and they don't come out for the ball," I told my players during a timeout, "there is no way we can lose."

Finally, with time running out, Kansas did come out for the ball. They had to foul our men and leave the hoop unguarded. We built our lead and won, 78–62.

After the game the Kansas coach spoke unhappily about "stall ball" and said there should be a thirty-second clock in college basketball.

I said I agreed. "I've been a fast-break man all my life," I told the press. "I didn't like what we had to do. I'm against stalling on purpose but here I had no choice. It's not a question of doing what you want or what is most appealing. That's irrelevant. You have to do what in your mind is most expedient within the present rules. The name of the game is Win."

We went on to beat Louisville and Army in two very physical games and advanced to the finals against Temple. The New York and Boston press were writing about Cousy going out on a blaze of glory, riding a nineteen-game winning streak, the longest in the nation. "A storybook finish for Cooz," one Boston reporter wrote.

I had thought that Kansas and Louisville were superior to us in talent. I believed that what had helped us to beat those two teams—and motivated the players through much of the streak—was a win-this-last-one-for-Cooz emotion. Billy Evans expressed the feeling to George Sullivan of the Boston *Herald-Traveler* on the eve of the final game: "Twenty years from now, when he talks about his great thrills of basketball and remembers Red Auerbach and Bill Russell and the Celtics, maybe he'll remember the team that won the NIT. I'd like that."

I was confident we could beat Temple. On paper we seemed pretty evenly matched. They had two excellent players in Eddie Mast and John Baum. But I thought we had more speed and quickness. At our last practice session, at a high school gym in New York, I told my players: "Maybe I'm making a mistake to tell you this, but I honestly feel you will beat Temple if you play your game. Only a phenomenal effort can beat you."

In the first half we got excellent shooting from Driscoll. But one of their stars, John Baum, was hitting, too. At the intermission we had only a small lead, 46–42.

I remember thinking as I walked toward the dressing room that things weren't going well. I had discovered that I could often sense a defeat, even when we were leading. In that first half we had looked tired, the effects of the two physical games against Louisville and Army showing. We were flat and only Driscoll's accuracy had kept us in the game.

The temptation was there: to walk into the dressing room and plead for one last half "to win this one for Cooz."

But I couldn't do it. We had come to the finals of the NIT winning for Cooz. I could have said the words but I would not have been honest with them. Winning for Cooz had helped us to beat better teams and get where we were. I could not in good conscience ask for more.

Six minutes into the second half we still led by five. Then Baum put in nine straight points and Temple went ahead. With six minutes left, we pulled to within one point and we had the ball. Driscoll wheeled for a hook— we seemed about to go ahead again. But he never got the shot off. The whistle blew and the official called a jump ball.

They got the tip, and that seemed to be the turning point. Temple picked up the pace and increased their lead. "Everyone just tired out at once," I thought as I watched my boys plod down the court. Temple won, 89–76.

After the game Terry was awarded the trophy as the tournament's Most Valuable Player. Then I was called out to center court with the team to receive our second-place trophy. The crowd gave me one last roar. There were tears in my eyes. Suddenly, my disappointment at losing was overcome by a sense of pride. My team had gone farther than anyone could have predicted. For a fleeting moment I thought that maybe Bill Flynn was right: you could be reasonably successful with good kids, playing within the rules. But I still wanted perfection, and "reasonably successful" wasn't good enough.

# LOOKING
# BACK

**W**hen I was first approached to write a book, I considered one that would be an exposé of recruiting in college basketball. But the more I thought about it, the more I realized others were better equipped to document the more sordid aspects of recruiting. Although we had bent a rule here and there, our program at Boston College had been reasonably honest. I had never really investigated what was going on at other schools; most of my information was secondhand. And I had been away from college coaching since 1969.

So I have tried to explain in this book how the pressures of college coaching affected one person and, by extension, how they must affect others in college athletics who are tying to be both successful and honest with themselves.

But I am able to add this postscript to my own experiences: from everything I have learned since I left college coaching, there are more recruiting violations than ever. And the reason is a basic one: money.

Recently the president of Notre Dame, Father Theodore Hesburgh, pointed out that the money made by Notre Dame football teams pays for the entire Notre Dame athletic program—every varsity sport. And there is money left over to pay for some academic programs. Without football, obviously, those other sports and those academic programs would be in trouble.

Notre Dame football makes money because Notre Dame teams win. Winning teams play in filled stadiums and attract television coverage. After turning down bowl invitations for years, the Notre Dame athletic department changed its mind in 1973. Bowl appearances mean extra income.

To win you need to recruit the talented players—the horses. "Recruiting is a justified pursuit, without question," Don Canham, the University of Michigan athletic director, told a New York *Times* reporter who was investigating recruiting. "Let me put it another way: It's a necessary evil. For instance, if we did not recruit and have great football teams . . . we wouldn't have any money. It's absolutely essential in our system of amateur athletics today. The recruited athlete is not only protecting the coach's job. He's supporting the whole ball of wax. . . ."

With so much at stake, you can imagine how hard the recruiters push to get those blue-chippers. A few years after I left BC, I was talking to a recruiter from a school in the Southwest. "You know how we get those kids from New York?" he said. "We send them across the border into Mexico to shack up for a few days. Every one of those kids signs on the dotted line when he gets back."

A recruiter for another Southwestern school told me,

"When we get kids down here to look over our campus, I give them a ride in a Lear jet that's owned by a friend of the school. We load the jet up with all kinds of goodies and send it up to 25,000 feet. When the jet lands a couple of hours later, the kids line up to sign. All they can think of is four more years of living like this."

Blue-chippers are invited each spring to "All-Star" tournaments—those flesh markets I mentioned earlier. While I was preparing this book, the promoter of one of those tournaments, who gets to know the blue-chippers intimately, told me that every kid who has played in his tournament during the past ten years has gone to a college that gave him something illegal.

I am amused that college officials are now screaming about the big, bad professional teams raiding college teams and even high schools for talent. In the most publicized case, the American Basketball Association took center Moses Malone right out of high school for a couple of million dollars, "stealing" him from the University of Maryland. The colleges scream that the pros are exploiting the kids. Yet the pros make legal, aboveboard offers. Some of the colleges make offers that are—by NCAA standards, anyway—illegal. And the colleges are after the same thing: to attract players who will create a winning team that will make money.

Some people don't want to hear any more about recruiting violations. "What is really wrong with recruiting?" they ask. "Some kid, often from the ghetto, gets a few dollars and an education. The college makes money to fund other sports. The fan sees good basketball. Everyone profits."

There are at least two answers to that attitude. The first is a moral argument. It's wrong to break the rules and it's wrong to teach young people that you can break the rules and get away with it. If a young man's teachers —his coaches, athletic directors, college presidents—are teaching him by example that the way to success is breaking or evading the rules, it is only logical for that young person to assume that this is the way other respected members of society conduct their lives and that this is the way he should conduct his own.

The other answer is that the recruiters don't always come through with their promises. A surprisingly small number of blue-chip players really get an education— among NBA players, fewer than half have college degrees even though the majority spent four years in college. Thousands of lesser players end up with neither a degree nor a career in pro ball.

Part of the misunderstanding has to do with statistics. Obviously, there are a few talented kids who take all the goodies offered by the college recruiter, go to a college and are chosen to All-America teams. Then they sign with the pros for a quarter of a million dollars or more. The visible few become pro stars and millionaires. No one is cheating them. But the following figures, from a New York *Times* survey on recruiting, tell you how few success stories there are.

Of some 200,000 seniors playing high school varsity basketball during a single season, only 5,700 of them will be playing college basketball as seniors. Some 200 of those will be drafted by the pros; of those, however, only some 50 will ever play more than a few minutes of pro ball.

And of those 50, only a handful—perhaps four or five—
will ever become stars or millionaires. So for a high school
senior there is about one chance in 4,000 of ever playing
pro ball and perhaps one chance in 40,000 of becoming a
Walt Frazier or Dave Cowens.

The burden of failure falls especially hard on the ambitious young black player who has fewer paths to success.
Dr. Roscoe Brown of the Institute for Afro-American Affairs of New York University uses strong language to
describe their experience: "Black youngsters pour too
much time and energy into sports. They're deluded and se-
duced by the athletic flesh peddlers, used for public
amusement—and discarded."

I agree with Dr. Brown. From what I have seen as a
college and pro coach, it is the black player, out of the
ghetto, who is more likely to be hurt by the recruiting system.

Lewis Schaffel is a New York lawyer who has helped
Tiny Archibald and other blacks to use their basketball
skills to lift themselves out of the ghetto. He has seen firsthand how the system works. "Most coaches are only interested in black kids who can be starters," he says. "They
don't want to recruit blacks who are going to be sixth,
seventh or eighth ballplayers. For one thing, the black kid
sitting on the bench becomes unhappy, thinking he isn't
getting the chance the Archibalds got to make the big
money in the pros. Secondly, by not recruiting black kids
for his bench, the coach can give scholarships to white
kids who'll give him a 'balanced' squad.

"But for the black kid who can start, coaches will offer
anything—new clothes, a car, a girl, anything. The kid is

shown a wonderful, wonderful weekend on campus. The kid signs. And during the next four years there is never again a weekend like that first one.

"The coach tells the kid: 'Show up for practice. If you've got any problems, see So-and-so. He's an alumnus and he'll take care of you.'

"But you can't take an eighteen-year-old black out of the South Bronx and stick him in the middle of Nebraska or Minnesota with white middle-class students and expect that he is going to grow. He is going to be homesick. He is going to be frightened. He is going to withdraw into his shell and stay there for the next four years.

"Coming from ghetto schools, many are not academically motivated. Often they lack the reading skills of the white kids from the suburbs who are now their classmates. That alone is both frightening and embarrassing.

"They may or may not go to classes. Even when they do, in that state of mind, what are they going to learn? Some of them seldom go to classes, figuring nobody at the school will care anyway, and often they're right. Whether they study or don't study, they're given grades that will get them by to play basketball.

"These kids need sympathetic guidance. They need someone who can teach them that there is more in life than a basketball, new clothes and a different girl each weekend. White blue-chippers need that guidance; many black kids need it more. But they don't get it from an angel interested only in keeping them happy with new clothes and from a coach who is interested in them only from three to five.

"The lucky ones last four years, although few of them ever get a diploma. The others leave a school and go to a smaller one, leave there and go somewhere else, ending up in the ghetto drinking out of a paper bag. Whatever chance they had to use their athletic talents to make it in a white man's world is wasted."

After I became a pro coach, I saw many of the "lucky ones" Schaffel mentions. They were the kids who had been the stars of their college teams, all-conference players who had been drafted by the pros. They would come to our preseason camp full of ambition and I would see that they weren't good enough for pro ball. As coach, I was the one who would have to cut them and end their basketball dreams.

This annual routine of cutting the rookies was the most heartrending task I ever had. I used to dread it every season and I was always tempted to say, "Check the list on the bulletin board. If your name is there, come back tomorrow. The rest of you, thanks for your time." But I couldn't do that.

He would come into my office looking apprehensive. I would be sitting behind a desk, looking at a twenty-three-year-old man-child. Up to this moment he has ridden through life atop a basketball, and that ball has kept him above the dirty, hard world of growing up black in America. Always there has been someone—coach, recruiter, agent— at his elbow, saying, I'll do this for you, I'll do that. Just show up for practice. Being human, the boy has believed the flattery and taken the path of least resistance. Who needs to study or go to class, he thinks, when basketball will always take care of me?

Now I have to say, "Son, I'm sorry, it's all over. You're not quick enough, your shot's not good enough. I'm going to have to let you go."

Talk about being frightened. He has lived his life with one object in mind—to play ball. Now here I am, a white man, telling him no. I have taken away the only vehicle he has for getting anywhere important in this world. "Get off the basketball," I seem to say, "and go back to the ghetto."

He breaks down and begins to cry. At least once I will break down myself during one of those scenes. A big center will look me straight in the face and say, "What the hell am I gonna do?" It's the most plaintive cry I have ever heard. *What the hell am I gonna do?*

And what about the handful of players, all products of the same system, who become rich and famous? What do they have to tell the millions of kids who admire and imitate them? Based on his experience in the recruiting environment, the superstar might well say this to kids: "Cheat. No one who wins, no one who succeeds, plays by the rules."

What are we creating with our addiction to success at any cost? The values of the recruiting system are not much different from those of the brilliant men who made the policies of the Vietnam war or the bright young men who never questioned orders in the Watergate affair. If winning is everything, then the end justifies the means. If we have to do a little cheating, a little secret bombing or some bugging and burglarizing in order to accomplish our goals, we should not be too finicky and we should try not to get caught.

The same mentality has shown up recently in even more unexpected areas. Some boy scout leaders were ordered to sign up more scouts in order to become eligible for federal funds. Under the pressure of time, some of the scout leaders found it too difficult to find real members. So they began adding fictional names—"ghost" boy scouts—to fill out the list and acquire additional money. At about the same time, it was revealed that a father had built a rigged car for his son to race in the Soap Box Derby. Then he swore that the boy had built the car all by himself. The boy won the race but the rigged car was discovered.

All of these people had good intentions—the father, the boy scout leaders, the Watergate men and the war-makers. All of them wanted to win. And yet somehow, as Jeb Magruder of Watergate fame has put it, the desire to win upset their moral compasses.

And the people in college athletics—from college president to assistant coach—have the best of intentions in trying to field winning teams. Colleges need contributions from alumni. Those contributions are often heaviest when the football or basketball team is number one. The college president knows what has to be done to win. But the president is locked into a situation. He needs the contributions that go with winning. A healthy university does a lot of good for a lot of people.

The college's athletic director knows what has to be done to win. But the athletic director is locked into a situation. If the team stops winning, box-office revenue will drop off and he won't have the money for such sports as golf, tennis and swimming, which do a lot of good for a lot of people.

The coach knows what has to be done to win. But the coach is locked into a situation. If the team loses, he is fired.

The assistant coach knows what has to be done to win.

But he too is locked into a situation. He is ambitious and wants a job as head coach someday. His performance here and the success of the team will determine his future. His position may be the worst of all. If recruiting violations are discovered, he is most likely to be involved or to have firsthand knowledge. He will be the first to be fired, while the others in the chain of command can disclaim responsibility for or knowledge of the violations. Yet the assistant may know that his superiors expect him to bend or break the rules discreetly.

I had the luxury of a free choice. But if I had been a coach with a big mortgage on the house, bills coming in that made the stomach sink, four kids to feed . . . and if I then had the choice between breaking a rule in the NCAA book and having a losing season and risking my job, I might well have broken the rule and tried like hell not to get caught.

We may all want to do the right thing, but we are not always allowed to. And therein lies the tragedy of this situation—not just for coaches but for all of us, no matter what our occupation, in a society where the bottom line is winning, succeeding, selling the product. All of us, too often, are boxed into positions where, even if we want desperately to stay honest, we cannot.

It seems to me that there are some relatively simple ways to reduce the cheating that is going on in college recruiting. Recently the NCAA has made real progress in tightening its regulations and enforcing them. But it must do a better job of what it is supposed to be doing: policing its members, especially in the ways they recruit. At this writing there are 669 member colleges of the NCAA playing basketball. The investigative staff was recently increased from four to twelve, but even this may be inadequate to police a highly competitive business. Some officials have suggested that the colleges contribute additional money to pay for more investigators. I agree with that. When there are more cops on the recruiting beat, there is going to be less cheating.

The National Association of Basketball Coaches has recommended stronger rules for the regulation of recruiting—and stronger penalties when those rules are violated. (Too often, recruiting violators have gotten off with a slap on the wrist.) I agree. If a blue-chipper knew he would lose his college eligibility by accepting an illegal offer, and if a coach knew he would lose his job by making an illegal offer, everyone would be, of necessity, more honest.

But the problem goes beyond better policing, and even beyond the world of college sports. From a broader point of view, I think a lot of us have to change our attitudes toward winning and losing. Winning is not the only thing and losers are not people who have something wrong with them. With my killer instinct, I'm the first to admit that changing these attitudes isn't easy. But I don't agree with the prominent coaches who see our country decaying because the will to win is dying. I see the danger on the other side. If the casualties of Vietnam and Watergate have not taught us that the end—winning—does not justify the means we use to win, then perhaps we will never learn.

# LOSING

# SAYING YES

I was tied up, a prisoner in a cellar. The people who had tied me up were going to kill me. I had to get away. I summoned all the strength in my arms and chest. I snapped the ropes. I bounded upward. I was running for my life. I flicked off a reaching hand. They were coming after me. I could hear them screaming. I collided with something. I smashed my way through it with my fists. I was running again, the screams louder behind me. I slammed into a blank wall.

I turned, trapped. My heart was pounding. There was no escape. They came at me. I swung at them with both fists. They were screaming . . .

. . . I awoke. I saw Missie standing in front of me. Her eyes were wide. She was pushing a blanket toward me. I looked down and understood why. I was naked and there was a ring of people staring at me.

I grabbed the blanket. I was standing in the driveway of our camp in New Hampshire. Around me were Missie and my two daughters, my mother-in-law, my partner and his wife, his two daughters and his mother-in-law. They were all breathing hard. I realized they had been my pursuers.

"Just another one of my nightmares," I said as offhandedly as I could.

But as we walked back to the house I could feel my heart pounding. It was going so fast I thought I might have a heart attack.

I was bleeding. There were small cuts and scratches all over me. I understood why when I saw how I had come flying out of the house. I had punched my way through a heavy screen door—naked, which is the way I usually sleep. And then, while running as fast as I could, I had slammed into that "blank wall"—actually a parked Buick—bloodying both my knees.

I had been having nightmares since I was a child, but this was the first time I had hurt myself. Several times, though, I had come close to hurting Missie. A few years after we were married, I tried to strangle an intruder who turned out to be Missie's leg. Only the arrival of a friend, who was sleeping next-door and heard the screaming, saved Missie from a post-midnight amputation. I always said that if I ever did away with her, I would have an alibi ready.

My Celtic roommate, Bill Sharman, had come to learn to live with my nightmares, although he was a little unnerved when I began screaming in French. One night I lashed out with my arm and knocked over a table lamp, which landed on Willie and cut his forehead. The next night I jumped up in bed, dreaming that there was an intruder sitting in the corner of the room.

"Don't you move, you son of a bitch," I screamed. "I see you there. Don't you move!"

I was groping for the switch on the table lamp. When I found it and flicked it on, the light woke me up. There was nothing in the corner of the room but a floor lamp.

I turned to look at Willie. He was huddled under a blanket, his head protected by his arms. As soon as he had heard me screaming, he had ducked for cover, figuring he was going to get clobbered again by that lamp.

At home, when I had a nightmare, I usually did nothing more active than leap out of bed. Missie would say, "What's the matter?" "Oh, just once around the bed," I'd say. I'd walk around the bed, eyes shut, still asleep, climb back into the bed and sleep the rest of the night.

Up to now my nightmares had been the family joke. But after that dash out of the house at camp—it happened late in the summer of 1956—I began to worry about having another nightmare that might be my last. I had already come within one turning of killing myself. If I had turned left instead of right after jumping out of bed, I would have smashed through another screen door and plunged some thirty feet onto rocks and water.

A month later to the day, while we were still at the camp, I had the same nightmare. I was tied down by people who wanted to kill me. Again I dreamed I had flung off the ropes. I flew out of the bed. Missie tried to stop me. I tossed her aside. I was running for my life.

Again I punched my way naked through that screen door. This time I sprinted down a rocky road, running as fast as I could. The road put blood blisters the size of silver dollars on the soles of my feet. At the end of the road I jumped behind some bushes. I picked up a broken limb. As I crouched low, I told myself I would clobber those people who were chasing me, screaming.

Fortunately, Missie's screams awoke me before I cracked her on the skull with that limb. Again she gave me a blanket and helped me back to the cabin, the usual gallery of spectators staring at this maniac who ran around in the night without any clothes on. Again there was blood flowing from cuts covering my body, and this time, in punching my way through that screen door, I had broken a finger.

I was very frightened. I had always believed I was capable of fighting back against anything that endangered me. But now I felt helpless. I realized that the moment I fell asleep I no longer had control of myself.

We were going to be at the camp for another two weeks. Each night I tied my wrists to the bed before I went to sleep. I thought about tying my legs too, but Missie advised me not to. "The way you fly out of that bed," she told me, "you'd take the bed with you. Or you'd break your back."

When we returned to Worcester, I went to see a psychiatrist. I told him about the two nightmares. He explained them to me this way:

"You'll notice that they have occurred during the off-season. During the season you are extremely active, flying here and flying there, playing one game after another. Then suddenly it all stops. You go up to your camp and suddenly your life is regimented—bugle blows at seven, breakfast at eight, hike at ten, and so on. It's a complete change from the free-lance, unstructured, competitive life you lead during most of the year. The camp routine makes you feel that you are tied down, that people are holding you, and you manifest this in your dream. Your subconscious is rejecting this regimentation and you have to run away."

He suggested I take a tranquilizer each night during the summers while I was at camp. The pills apparently worked and I didn't have any more of those midnight flights through screen doors.

When I decided to quit coaching early in 1969, however, I was a little worried. For the first time in my life, I was going to be living a regimented life for twelve months a year. The lack of competition was going to leave a tremendous void.

I expressed that concern during an interview with a New York writer, Larry Merchant, a few days before my final game with Boston College against Temple in Madison Square Garden. We were talking about my leaving basketball.

"Maybe," I said to Merchant, "you cannot hone your life to a competitive edge for twenty-five years and just drop it. The withdrawal symptoms must be horrendous."

But I wasn't going to drop competition, not yet.

While I was in New York for the NIT, I got a phone call from George Mikan, who was then the Commissioner of the American Basketball Association. George asked me if I would be interested in coaching the New York Nets. I also got a phone call from Sam Cohen, a friend who was the sports editor of the Boston *Record-American*. Sam asked me to call a Max Jacobs. At the time I didn't know who Jacobs was. When I inquired, I learned that he was the owner of a multi-million-dollar empire that included the Cincinnati Royals of the NBA. Jacobs wanted to talk to me about coaching the Royals.

I told both the Nets and Jacobs that I would be happy to sit down with them, but I was reasonably certain that I would say no to both of them. I had enjoyed coaching twenty-five or thirty games a season at BC. I knew I could not possibly enjoy coaching a hundred, as I would have to do as a pro coach. Also, I would have to spend much of the year away from Worcester. Our older daughter, Marie, was starting college nearby in Boston, so we'd be separated from her. And we'd have to take our younger girl, Tish, out of school and put her in another one that she might not like. Then, there was all that traveling—half of your life, it sometimes seemed, spent cooped up in an airplane.

The Nets made a very attractive offer. I considered it for a short while and then said thanks but no.

Max Jacobs was harder to turn down. Max was in his early thirties. He was well dressed but not mod, dynamic but not overbearing. He knew how to talk, but he also knew how to listen. He and his brother, Jeremy, had inherited the multi-million-dollar empire from their father, who had started the business out of a pushcart in Brooklyn. Now the Jacobs brothers operated food concessions in sports arenas around the world. Max used to say that he was nothing more than a "peanuts and popcorn salesman," which was obviously something of an understatement.

I liked him. He had a flair for the dramatic. Before he took over his father's business he had been an actor, performing some Shakespearean roles among other things. And he was tireless. I learned later that he worked seven days a week, twelve to sixteen hours a day, keeping in daily contact with the people who ran all of his enterprises. He also was deeply interested in the problems of the Middle East. In 1975 he would send an elaborate proposal called "Framework for Peace" to Secretary of State Henry Kissinger and other world leaders.

We talked in New York and later in Worcester. Max kept making his offer more and more attractive. At one point I said to my lawyer, "No matter what we ask for, Max says yes."

The package included a salary of more than $100,000 a year for three years. The money would be invested for me. Assuming the market went up, I would be financially secure after three years, able to do whatever I wanted to do, creatively or otherwise, with the rest of my life.

As a player I had never earned more than $35,000 a season. Still, I had managed to use my basketball fame to make money in other business ventures. Even though I hadn't been paid what today's players are making, I was a kid from an East Side ghetto who made a lot of money playing a child's game. I owned a big house and I was living comfortably. How could I complain?

But that ghetto background had done to me what it had done to many of my contemporaries. It had left me with a tendency to be frugal and a lifelong concern about being financially secure. When you are born poor, as Joe Gara-giola once put it, you are always poor. So when Max Jacobs said, in effect, "Bob, you will never have to worry about money again," I listened.

While I was considering Max's offer, I went to see Arnold Auerbach and asked his advice.

"Why don't you wait?" he asked. "Russell is thinking of quitting. And if he does, you can probably have the Celtic job."

The trouble was, I had a $100,000-a-year contract in my pocket—probably the largest ever offered an NBA coach—and an immediate decision was necessary. I said thanks to Arnold and went back to trying to make up my mind.

If I took the job, I knew Missie and the girls would go along. I don't think it had ever been stated in the house but it was understood: Daddy's career came first. Everything revolved around what I had to do—as a player who had to be rested and ready for games, later as a so-called superstar who had to go around the country to make speeches and personal appearances, and then as a coach.

I knew that the girls had missed my not being at home as often as most fathers. Once, when I was a player, I had to stay home for a week because of a charley horse. After the team came back from a road trip, my older daughter Marie met Arnold before a game. He asked how I was.

"All right," she said, "but now we're hoping he breaks a leg so he can stay home even longer."

On the other hand, it was hard to resist the money—and the challenge. I had turned the Boston College team around. Now I would be going into another situation with turn-around potential. For years the Royals had been a team never at the top of the NBA, never at the bottom, usually hanging at the .500 level. Maybe I could start them upward.

And, of course, I would be competing again, with no need to worry about withdrawal symptoms and nightmares.

I said yes to Max.

# STARTING OUT

I may have been a babe in the woods when I went to Boston College, but I took the Cincinnati job with no illusions about why Max Jacobs was paying me more than $100,000 a year. I wasn't being paid for my coaching genius, nor for whatever success I had attained as a college coach—there were other college coaches who had been more successful. I was hired because I was a "name," and Max knew that if there was any basketball interest in Cincinnati it would have to be reawakened by a name that would get everybody's attention.

Around the NBA, Cincinnati had never been considered a good basketball town—small crowds coming to an old arena a good way out of town. At home the Royals seldom drew more than 6,000 bodies to a building that held 12,000. The building, incidentally, was owned by Max Jacobs. He needed the Royals to keep it reasonably filled for forty-one dates a season, and this explained why the team was still in Cincinnati.

When Max hired me, he also hired a new general manager, Joe Axelson, and he told both of us, "I will leave you two guys alone. You are the experts, you make the decisions. Whatever moves you two decide to make, they will have my approval. I don't expect any miracles. All I ask is that you keep me informed."

That carte blanche was one of the most appealing aspects of the job as far as I was concerned.

I met Axelson when I flew out to Cincinnati shortly after I signed the contract with Max. Joe was about my age, in his early forties. His father had been a very successful high school basketball coach in the Midwest, and Joe had coached while he was in the service. For the past ten years or so he had worked with the National Association for Intercollegiate Athletics in administering athletic programs. He was making a big leap from college sports to the NBA. Where he had been dealing with amateurs, he would now be negotiating multi-million-dollar contracts with players and their agents. But Joe had a brilliant mind, and a reputation for being a good administrator and smart promoter.

I found him warm and gregarious, with a good sense of humor, and we shared, among other things, a liking for Chinese food after games. Many coach–general manager relationships are fraught with conflict, the GM suspecting that the coach wants to get away from his win-or-perish pressures by taking the GM's job. But Joe knew I had no desire to be a general manager. So we had a good relationship, each trusting the other.

I brought an assistant coach with me to Cincinnati. He was Draff Young, a former college guard whose brother had played with the Harlem Globetrotters. Draff himself had toured for a while with Marquis Haynes, the former Globetrotter.

I met Draff when he was a promotion man for Randolph Manufacturing, which made Bob Cousy basketball shoes. Draff and I worked together on promotions. Newspaper ads would tell kids there was going to be a Bob Cousy foul-shooting contest at a shopping center, and at the scheduled time we would swoop in by car—sometimes even by helicopter. Draff ran the contest while I went inside the store and gave out autographed pictures. Then I would pose for photos with the contest winners and we would swoop off to some other center. I knew that Draff's promotional talent and experience would be helpful to the Royals.

Draff also knew basketball talent, having been around it with Haynes and the Globetrotters, and he knew most of the black players in the NBA and ABA. As my assistant, he would spend most of his time on the road, looking at college talent. When he was with the team, he would assist me at practices or on the bench during games. I also thought Draff could be a conduit between the black players and me. This was the first time I would be coaching a predominantly black team. If the players had problems that they were reluctant to discuss with a white coach, I thought they might feel freer to bring them to Draff.

Looking at the Royals, who had won forty-one and lost forty-one the previous season, I thought we had three genuine NBA players. One was Tom Van Arsdale, a forward who could also play guard—a guy who came dedicated to play and who could have been a superstar if he had been two inches taller. Then there were our two bread-and-butter players: Jerry Lucas and Oscar Robertson. Both were home-grown, Jerry having been an All-America at Ohio State and Oscar at the University of Cincinnati. Lucas was potentially a great forward with a good shooting touch and with the height to be a top rebounder. Oscar was one of the two or three greatest guards in the NBA, then or ever. There were two young players—a guard, Herman Gilliam, and a forward, Fred Foster—who I thought had the potential to be NBA starters. The rest were players who were hanging on the edge of the NBA.

Before I came to Cincinnati, I had heard rumors that there was friction between Jerry and Oscar. People told me: "They can't stand one another. Jerry is selfish, Oscar holds the ball too much."

I had always believed the best way to handle that kind of a problem was to bring it out into the open. I am like almost everyone else: I don't like unpleasant confrontations. But at BC I had learned to force myself to bring a player into my office when I thought something was bothering him, sit him down, and say, "Whatever the problem is, let's get it out on the table." And I found that ten or fifteen minutes of airing the problem would usually make it vanish.

I flew out to Cincinnati to meet the local press. I asked Jerry and Oscar, who were at the conference, to come with me after it was over into a private room. We sat down.

"Look," I said, "the rumor in the league is that there is friction between the two of you. Is there anything to what I hear?"

Both said much the same thing: "That's all overdone, we get along fine."

I believed them and never did see any friction between them. I wasn't as concerned with what they said, however, as with letting them know I was concerned about exposing and solving any problem that might exist.

All during that summer and fall of 1969, Joe and his staff put on an intensive promotional campaign tied to my coming to Cincinnati. Several times I flew out to assist in the campaign, doing TV and radio shows and making myself available for interviews. At one press conference I announced I was coming back as a player. I didn't plan to play any more than a few minutes here and there, but Joe and I were hoping that the comeback of Cousy would help at the box office.

That fall Max sold the radio broadcasting rights to the Royals games. The year before there had been no radio coverage. And he managed to increase the team's local TV exposure. This pleased him and it pleased me. I was eager to justify my record salary. In those days I often stated publicly that I was being overpaid. However, my opinion would change over the years and any guilt I felt about the money eventually vanished.

In the early fall of 1969, Missie and I left Worcester for Cincinnati. Although we would be back in six or eight months, both of us felt some trauma. We had been living there since our marriage in 1950. Missie would be separated from her sister, whom she was used to seeing two or three times a week, and we would both miss our close friends.

We left Marie at college in Boston. Tish came with us to Cincinnati, where she enrolled in public school. She made friends very quickly and did well in school, which relieved both Missie and me.

Our training camp was at the Cincinnati Gardens. During the first few days at camp, I thought, *We've got more rebuilding to do than I realized.* The team looked far worse in person than it did in game films.

I knew what kind of team I wanted: a team that played strong defense, controlled its own backboard and ran the fast break, with everything else kept as simple as possible. To me this is the only way to win in the NBA.

What I saw at the training camp was a team that had deficiencies in many areas. It didn't have quite enough speed, it didn't play strong defense, it didn't control the boards. It looked like a team that lost as often as it won.

I cut people and brought in others. One day I got a phone call from Johnny Green, a veteran forward who had been cut by Philadelphia. I had played against him and knew he was a six-foot-five forward who could leap higher than most people six-ten.

But John was also thirty-six years old, and the team that signed him would have to pay some $20,000 into the pension fund. I invited him to come to our camp. In his first practice with us, he stood head and shoulders over all our other forwards. He knew the fast break and showed the most amazing dexterity and body control that I have ever seen in a man his size. Joe Axelson and I concluded that Green was worth the $20,000 gamble. We thought he could be a significant addition to the team, and as it happened we were right.

Near the end of the pre-season, we played the Chicago Bulls. They had a rookie guard who caught my eye as being quick and fast and who played aggressive defense. I liked him so much that a few days after the game we concluded a trade with Chicago to get him, giving up Walt Wesley, a center. The rookie guard's name was Norm Van Lier, and he turned out to be the player I admired more than any I ever coached.

Our first regular season game was at home, against the New York Knicks, who would go on to win the NBA championship that 1969–70 season. On the day of the game we ran newspaper ads with a photo of me in uniform and under the photo the headline WOULD YOU BELIEVE?

Actually, as the ad went on to explain, I could not play since Arnold Auerbach had insisted that he still owned the playing rights to me. Technically, I still belonged to the Celtics. But we thought that the months of promotional effort, climaxed by these ads, would attract a reasonably large crowd to see my debut as an NBA coach.

We attracted fewer than 6,000 people, just about the average for the previous season. That was disappointment number one. Disappointment number two was the game. We led the Knicks, 88–87, with two and a half minutes to go. Then we committed a series of errors and the Knicks beat us, 94–89.

In the locker room I chewed on a dead cigar. The reporters recalled Arnold Auerbach's habit of lighting up a cigar when the Celtics had clinched a game. Our next contest was against the Celtics and one reporter said, "Maybe you'll light up your first victory cigar in Boston."

I wanted to win this game against the Celtics for several reasons. We had been terrible all during the exhibitions, and we'd lost our first game. I didn't want to get into a losing rut. And, of course, the Celtics were my old team. "Everyone likes to do well when he goes home to perform in front of his friends," I told the writers in Boston. "Naturally I want to do well here, in a place I consider home and in front of people I consider friends."

When I came out onto the floor for the pregame warmups, the crowd stood and gave me an ovation. The photographers posed Celtic coach Tommy Heinsohn (Russell had retired), Arnold and me together. I kidded with Arnold about not giving me my release to play for the Royals and there was a lot of good-natured laughter.

But I was more nervous than I had been before my first game in Cincinnati. By the fourth period I was down on one knee, clutching a scorecard. We were losing by twelve, 89–77. Then John Green made our gamble on him begin to look good by contributing eleven points within three minutes. We were now within a point of the Celtics, 91–90.

Heinsohn called a time-out and talked to his players. They began to hit the hoop again. But Oscar and John kept us even, and we tied the score at 103–103 with three minutes left. Then Oscar put in two important baskets, giving us a 109–106 lead, with less than a minute to go. We held on and walked off the floor with a 110–108 victory.

An hour or so later we were lifting off from the Boston airport. I thought to myself, *I'm competing again and I've just won for the first time as an NBA coach.* It seemed like a good start.

# LEARNING
# THE
# TRADING GAME

I was sitting in my office after practice one day early in that first season when Jerry Lucas came by. Jerry had been a superstar at Ohio State, playing on the same team with John Havlicek. John had gradually developed into one of the great players in the league, but Lucas had never really progressed. In seven years in the league, he had never become the superstar he might have been. To me he was typical of dozens of players I would later coach in the NBA—a guy with massive individual ability who used maybe only 80 percent of it. Luke came to play basketball the way a lot of people go to the office: they punch in at nine, sip coffee and eye the clock, then leave promptly at five. Luke would often sit in the locker room before a game and talk about his fast-food business. I thought he lacked that inborn competitive spirit, the killer instinct, that you need to excel in an emotional game like basketball. I just couldn't imagine Luke stepping on somebody's face after stealing a ball.

In my office that day, we chatted for a while, neither of

us saying very much of importance. But I sensed there was something he wanted to say and I finally asked him what was on his mind.

"Bob," he said, "I don't think I can play defense the way you want me to play it."

I nodded. Jerry had bad knees that limited his mobility. "What do we do, Jerry?"

He said he would like to be traded to San Francisco. I told him I would see what we could do.

Joe Axelson and I talked over a possible trade for Lucas. We knew some fans would be unhappy if we traded him, but Luke had several strikes against him. First, in good years and bad, he had not put the bodies in the seats here in Cincinnati. If he had been that kind of superstar, we might never have let him go.

Second, I had concluded that Jerry wasn't physically or psychologically capable of playing the fast-breaking offense and aggressive defense I wanted. I didn't want to bring in young players who might absorb his attitude. Within reason I wanted my players to come to a game talking basketball.

We checked around the league for possible trades. As luck would have it, the only team that showed any great interest in Jerry was San Francisco, where he wanted to go. We asked for Jeff Mullins, a six-foot-four guard who was averaging twenty-two points a game.

Instead of Mullins, San Francisco offered Jimmy King, a playmaking guard who had made the All-Star team the previous season, and Bill Turner, a young six-foot-seven forward. Turner had shown a lot of promise, I had been told, during his first two seasons in the league, but I had never seen him play. San Francisco was coming east to play Atlanta and New York that week, so I told Draff Young to follow the team and scout Turner.

The Warriors beat Atlanta by a point in the first game. Draff called me and said that Turner had scored something like twenty-eight points. As I recall, he was the team's high scorer. The next night, in New York, San Francisco beat the Knicks. Again, right after the game, Draff phoned me. "There was only one player on the floor tonight for San Francisco," he told me. "You won't believe this, but it was Turner."

The next morning we got a telephone call from the San Francisco general manager, Bob Feerick. "Look," he told us, "we've been talking about this for a week now. The deal still stands: Lucas for Jimmy King and Bill Turner. But the team is on its way back to San Francisco and we've got to make a decision before the plane lands."

Feerick claimed that Franklin Mieuli, the owner of the team, was a great admirer of Jimmy King. "He thinks Jimmy is a hell of a kid," Feerick said. "If that plane lands in San Francisco before we can make a deal, someone is going to leak it to the kid and the kid is going to run to Mieuli. He'll talk Mieuli out of it. So we have to make the deal while the plane is in the air."

We took the bait. While that plane was somewhere over the continent, we traded Lucas for Jimmy King and Bill Turner.

We had hoped that Turner could be the big, young, high-scoring forward we needed. He never turned out to be that kind of player, nor, to my recollection, did he ever again perform like he did in those games against Atlanta and New York. He had all the assets you look for in a forward, but when the whistle blew he didn't function at an NBA level.

Jimmy King refused to report to us until we gave him a new contract. We gave him the contract, but in his second game for us he injured an ankle. He was out two months. When he came back late in the season, he played very little. And the following season, 1970–71, he couldn't win a starting job. "I'm sorry, Jimmy," I told him. "I have to cut you. We can't be paying this kind of money for someone sitting on the bench."

By any standard we came out on the short end of that deal. We should have held out for Mullins or tried to trade Lucas elsewhere. Joe Axelson and I were new to this trading game, however, and looking back I think we let Bob Feerick do a little hustle job on us. But I still think we were right in letting Lucas go.

Telling players that we were letting them go—traded, cut, put on waivers, whatever—was a task I had suspected would be difficult for someone as emotional as I am. And it was.

I had seen enough trades to understand how the traded player feels: he has been rejected. It's like a wife telling a husband or a boss telling a long-time employee: "I don't want you around any more."

A lot of fans don't realize that a player can tie himself emotionally to a team every bit as strongly as a fan. A player comes out of Holy Cross, whose uniform he has worn for four years, and now he puts on the uniform of the Boston Celtics. The player transfers his loyalty to that Celtic uniform. This is his new alma mater, his new parent figure. For five or ten years the organization gives him a sense of identity and importance, as well as a handsome income. The local fans come out to cheer him on. The player, only naturally, feels affection for the organization and the fans. They have been good to him, he wants to be good to them.

Then one day the telephone rings. Calling is a voice from the organization: "We're letting you go. You're going somewhere else and we're getting someone else to replace you."

The uncertainties can be frightening: *Are they letting me go because I'm not good enough any more? Am I finished? Will I be able to prove myself all over again in front of strange faces?*

Such uncertainties are especially unsettling for the older player. So I knew Adrian Smith was going to take it hard when we decided to trade him in December of that first season. Odie, as everyone called him, was now thirty-three years old. He had been with the Royals since 1961. In his prime he had been a top-notch guard, but now he was playing only six or seven minutes a game. Norm Van Lier was working very well with Oscar Robertson in the backcourt. I couldn't see much of a future for Odie with us, especially since I hoped to make the team faster.

We asked around the league and again only San Francisco showed any interest. They offered a second-round draft choice in return. That was good enough for us. Odie was earning around $35,000 a year, too high a salary (at least at that time) for someone playing only a few minutes a game. We said yes to San Francisco. They were coming to Cincinnati to play us on Christmas Day, and they suggested that we make the trade before that game.

Joe and I decided to try and wait until after the game to make the announcement. I called Bob Feerick. "Look," I said, "I can't ruin Odie's Christmas. Let me tell him about the trade after the game on Christmas Day. Unless we get into foul trouble and I have to use him, I'll keep him on the bench. And I'll tell him about the trade right after the game."

Feerick agreed. As it turned out, the game went into overtime, I was short on guards, and I had to use Odie. But San Francisco couldn't have minded too much since they won, 124–120.

Then I called Odie into my office and told him about the trade. I wasn't surprised when he broke down and started to cry. I was close to tears myself. As with every player I traded, I tried to explain that there was nothing personal involved, that we liked him and appreciated all he had done for the team, but I was making the trade because I needed to build a younger and speedier team.

We shook hands and left on good terms. Odie, I am sure, understood what I had to do and I understood how Odie felt, suddenly let go.

I heard later that Odie's wife was angry at me for months after the trade. She never spoke to me, so I don't know what her feelings were. I had learned as a player, however, that wives sometimes take the ups and downs of the game harder than their husbands. They fret when their husbands sit on the bench. And a trade is even harder, since it often means that the family is uprooted and that the player's livelihood may be in jeopardy.

I will never forget that trade for two reasons. One is the emotional strain of having to break the news to a nice guy like Odie. The other is the second-round draft choice that we got for Odie. We thought very little of that choice at the time. Second-round picks are not likely to become starters and we didn't even know whom we would choose.

But he turned out to be the man who, more than anyone, would turn the team around.

Early in December of 1969 we had made another trade. This time I was one of the players involved. I had wanted to come back to play but Arnold Auerbach was insisting that Cincinnati give up something for the playing rights to Bob Cousy.

"Look," I told Arnold several times, "I'm only going to be playing a few minutes a game. What can I be worth? And when we come to Boston my being in uniform may even put a few more bodies into the seats for you."

But Arnold wouldn't be rushed into anything. Even though I was forty-one years old, and not likely to be worth much, he insisted he would not give away the rights to me for nothing. Finally we agreed on a trade: we gave up Bill Dinwiddie, a forward who didn't figure to play very much for us, in exchange for me.

I had worked out all summer and scrimmaged with the players during training camp. When I entered my first game as a Royal, I became the oldest guy, before or since, to play in the NBA. John Green was delighted. He was no longer the old man of the team. In the locker room after a practice he'd pat me on the back, showing a lot of solicitude. "You did all right, Bob," he'd tell me. "You were really keeping up with us young fellows."

Actually, according to the NBA Guide, I appeared in only seven games for a total of thirty-four minutes. In only one game did I play any significant role. The Knicks came to town with a fifteen-game winning streak. With about ninety seconds remaining, Oscar fouled out of the game. We were ahead, 101–98. I put myself in.

Both teams scored and we led, 103–100. A few moments later I was fouled by Bill Bradley. I put in two free throws and we were up by five, 105–100, with twenty seconds remaining. It seemed that we would break the Knick streak—a big accomplishment for us.

The Knicks got the ball in to Willis Reed. Tom Van Arsdale fouled Willis, who dropped in a pair of free throws. We led, 105–102, with sixteen seconds remaining.

I called a time-out so we could bring the ball in near midcourt. I passed the ball in to Van Arsdale but Dave DeBusschere stepped very aggressively in front of Tommy, stole the pass and scored. They were behind by only a point, 105–104, but we had the ball.

Tommy started to bring the ball up for us against a New York press. Reed got a finger on the ball and tapped it to Walt Frazier. Van Arsdale had to foul Frazier to prevent a basket. But then Walt put in both free throws, and we went off 106–105 losers.

It was a tough loss and I went away from it feeling two burdens: one as a player who had come in and helped lose the game with a bad pass, the other as the coach who had sent me in.

In fact, I had put myself into the game with great reluctance. But I saw nobody on the bench who I thought would keep cool enough in that kind of situation. *Whatever I do or don't do out there*, I remember thinking as I took off my jacket, *at least I'll keep my cool*.

What was happening to me, I believe, can happen to any aging superstar who becomes a player-coach. When a critical situation comes up during a game, one side of you tells you to withdraw yourself from it. You know your wheels are not what they used to be, that you can't function as you once did. You don't want to let down the team nor do you want to hurt your image. But another side of you tends to push you toward going into the game. You know the players and fans want you to go in there, hoping you can do for them what you used to be able to do.

So you're torn: Should you put yourself in or should you withdraw? For a coach a decision like that is an added burden. Generally speaking, I think most player-coaches do what I began to do, tending to withdraw and to use themselves less and less.

Shortly after that New York game, Max Jacobs reminded me that by coming back as a player I had made myself eligible for the players' pension. I had forgotten about the pension. It hadn't existed when I was a player, although I had worked hard for its establishment as the first president of the NBA Players Association.

I found that if I would contribute about $20,000 to make up for the years since I retired from the Celtics, I could collect about $10,000 a year at age sixty-five. But then, while I was considering whether to put in the $20,000, I heard what some bad-mouths were saying around the league.

"Cousy's not so dumb," the stories went. "He wasn't eligible for the pension fund, so as a coach he puts a uniform on himself and plays a few minutes here and there. He's found a way to make himself $10,000 a year when he's sixty-five."

I frankly resented this gossip. I had not come back to qualify for the pension. But if I did qualify, I felt I would deserve it after my years in the league. I became stubborn —maybe stupid—and quit as a player without qualifying. As a former coach, I'll collect about $1,200 a year at age sixty.

# OSCAR
# AND THE
# DRAFT

**M**idway through the 1969–70 season, we were flying back from a game in Boston. The team had been playing reasonably well, and Oscar Robertson was our leading scorer with about twenty-five points a game. The league was then split into two divisions. We were in the Eastern Division and were only a game out of fourth place. If we finished fourth, we'd make the playoffs.

Oscar had played the entire game in Boston, but on the plane he told our trainer, "I can't play tomorrow night. I pulled a groin muscle."

Every NBA coach knows that he must find the time to give his players a rest. There are just too many games for any but a handful of men to play every minute. When I was with the Celtics near the end of my career, Arnold would occasionally allow me a couple of extra days to recuperate from an injury, especially when the few days off might help me get ready for the playoffs.

Now I was faced with Oscar's injury. I was upset because the timing was so bad. Other players could sit out a few games without serious consequences to the team. But he was half our offense—his absence would be felt at a time when we were still in contention for a playoff spot. I was the last one in the world to want him to play if he was seriously hurt, but I knew that a pulled groin muscle is difficult to diagnose. Even if Oscar wasn't seriously hurt, we would have to take his word about how bad it was and how long it would take to heal.

I decided to take this opportunity to make two points to Oscar. One was that we would not ask him to play when he was injured—in fact, we would take extra precautions to assure that he remained in top condition. The other point was that in injury situations the team doctor and I would remain in control.

When we got back to Cincinnati, I asked our team doctor to examine him.

"What do you think?" I asked afterward. "Is it serious enough to keep him out?"

As I expected, the doctor said it was hard to tell.

"Assuming he has a serious pull, how long would it take him to recover completely?"

The doctor said a minimum of two to three weeks.

We agreed to announce that Oscar would be out of action for two to three weeks to give the injury plenty of time to heal and to prevent the chance of further complications. I suspected that perhaps two weeks was longer than Oscar wanted to stay out. But even though it would be to the team's advantage on the floor to have him back sooner, I thought it important to make my point to him and to the others on the team.

Two weeks later Oscar came back and played from the

start at his customary high level. I was happy to have him back, and as far as I know, he was happy to be back.

Inevitably, of course, we were compared: who was the better guard, Cousy or Robertson? It seems to me that stars in any sport are difficult to compare. The good athlete adjusts his skills to his circumstances. I developed as a playmaking guard on a team that had a succession of excellent shooters. Oscar developed as a scorer partly because he played on a weaker offensive team during his years at Cincinnati. When he went to Milwaukee, he became more of a playmaker because those skills were valuable on a team with a big center like Jabbar. Similarly, if I had been on a weaker offensive team, I might have done more shooting and developed into a scorer.

As a person and as a player, Oscar came at most people with a distant, sophisticated attitude. He is, I think, a cut or two above most people intellectually, and is very much aware of racial problems in this country. Oscar seemed to deal with these problems, at least when I knew him, by keeping himself especially aloof in his dealings with the white world.

He often displayed a chip on his shoulder toward the Establishment. One day a member of Joe Axelson's staff asked Norm Van Lier to make a personal appearance to help us sell season tickets. Norm agreed. The promotion man gave him the details and left.

Oscar had been listening to the conversation. He walked over to Norm and said, "What are they giving you for that?"

In games, he carried that same chip on his shoulder toward referees. No one could look more startled than Oscar when a foul was called on him. It was often said that he went through his career absolutely certain that he had never committed a foul.

However, he did not show the same hostility in his relationship with me—or any other coach, as far as I know. He listened carefully, said very little and did whatever I asked of him. The younger players looked up to him. Like some superstars who can do things relatively easily, he sometimes became impatient when others could not. During practice he could blast a player and leave the guy in a state of shock.

Oscar's confidence and talent made him a coach's dream. When you needed two points, you could tell him to take the ball and go one-on-one and he would get you a hoop more often than not. He played with a sureness that no one could stop him from doing what he wanted to do. He was a professional and I respected him for it.

Late in that first season, Joe and I sat down and looked at our plans to build a winning team. Comparing what we had with what we needed, we gradually came to the conclusion that we should trade Oscar. We both knew how important he had been to the Royals, but there were many points in favor of a trade.

First, we desperately needed strength on our forward wall. Lucas was gone, Turner had been disappointing, and John Green was getting old. By contrast, Norm Van Lier was our most promising young player. He was already showing that he could take over part of Oscar's backcourt job—running the offense.

Second, our attendance was still disappointing. Like

Lucas, Oscar didn't seem to be the kind of star who could draw the fans, at least not in Cincinnati. Yet we had heard that when his contract expired at the end of the season, he would be asking for a three-year contract at something like $200,000 a year.

Looking around the league for a suitable trade, Joe and I learned that Gus Johnson of Baltimore was having differences with his front office. The Bullets were willing to trade him even-up for Oscar. Every time we weighed this deal, it came out in our favor. The two of them were equal in age and talent, but Johnson had the skills as a forward that could turn us around. He could rebound and score. And he would play for less money than Oscar.

As soon as Baltimore agreed to the deal, I personally phoned Oscar and told him that we had been talking to Baltimore about a trade that involved him. We met that morning in the office of our attorney, Bro Lindhorst, and explained the terms to Oscar and his lawyers.

Soon after the meeting, however, Oscar let it be known that he wouldn't go to Baltimore. He invoked a clause in his contract giving him the right to approve any trade. And he added that he would not play another season in Cincinnati.

I couldn't argue with Oscar's legal right to approve the trade. I agreed that veteran stars should have some say about where they might be traded. But I didn't go as far as baseball's Curt Flood, who claimed that pro athletes were treated like "chattels." Nobody likes to be traded, but I always thought—and still do—that when a new team offers a superstar a salary in six figures, the money could take the sting out of any trade. Their incomes

seemed to disqualify Flood or Robertson from being anybody's chattel.

Later I sat down and talked to Oscar. I explained my
position and tried to persuade him to reconsider his. "But
if you won't go to Baltimore," I concluded, "then we'll
have to make the best deal we can for you."

Oscar sat and listened. He thanked me and left. But he
didn't change his mind: he was not going to Baltimore.

Now a new development complicated the situation. We
learned that Mike Storen, then the general manager of the
Indianapolis franchise in the American Basketball Association, wanted to sign Oscar. Oscar would have to sit out
for a year, but there was a rumor that the ABA would
pay him for the year off and we worried that Oscar might
agree. If he went to the ABA, we would get nothing for
him.

This threat rushed us into a decision. Milwaukee let us
know that they would trade for Oscar, and Oscar said he
would go. The Bucks offered us the pick of any two players on their roster, with one notable seven-foot-one exception. We needed a big strong forward—a Gus Johnson
type—to build up our front wall, so we picked Charlie
Paulk, a six-nine forward who had been chosen fourth in
the draft two years earlier. Since then he had been in the
service, but all reports we received said he was a top prospect with good mobility and a fine outside shot. We also
took the Bucks' top guard, Flynn Robinson, who usually
scored twenty points or more when he played us.

Early in the following season we saw that Charlie
Paulk could not perform at an NBA level. Off the court
Charlie was a nice, happy-go-lucky young man and he

went on being nice when the whistle blew; people pushed him around. Flynn Robinson was also disappointing. I saw that while Flynn had the speed to fit into our fast break, he wasn't able to absorb coaching.

These disappointments were embarrassing because they left us open to the charge that we had given Robertson away without getting anything in return. Joe Axelson and I felt that maybe we had been too hasty, allowing the threat of Oscar's jumping to the ABA to hurry us into the Milwaukee trade. But even if we had made the trade we wanted—for Gus Johnson—we would have ended up paying for a lot of medical bills. Gus hurt his knee and was never again the overpowering forward he had been. So people with twenty-twenty hindsight would still have said we made a mistake. Trading is an unpredictable business.

While the arrangements were being made for the Oscar trade, we were also thinking about the college draft. By March, we knew we had no chance of finishing fourth and getting into the playoffs. We and Boston were stepping on each other's heels in a race for fifth place. If we could finish ahead of Boston, I thought, it would be a big psychological boost for the team. On the other hand, if we finished behind, we had an excellent chance of drafting the center we needed—Dave Cowens.

Dave was from the Cincinnati area and was playing college ball for Florida State. From what Draff and I had seen of him, we thought he had the speed, quickness and strength to become a first-rate center in the NBA, even though he was relatively small at six-foot-nine.

Dave knew we had been scouting him. In fact, he wrote

me a letter, saying in substance, "Dear Coach Cousy, I know you are interested in me, but I would appreciate it if you would not draft me, as I am not interested in playing in Cincinnati."

Well, I thought, neither are a lot of other players. But we knew that if we drafted him he would have to play for us since he had already signed a league contract. (The NBA was guaranteeing that he would not go to the ABA.) And we knew the salary he had agreed to and were willing to pay it.

We had learned that we had a chance at Cowens by talking to the teams ahead of us in the draft. Detroit was interested in Bob Lanier. San Diego had not made up its mind but didn't mention Dave, and neither did San Francisco. We assumed that one of these teams would pick Pete Maravich.

Either we or Boston would probably draft fourth, depending on who finished lower in the standings. I knew Arnold Auerbach had been looking at Cowens, but he was also interested in a center from New Mexico State named Sam Lacey. I liked Lacey myself, but I liked Cowens better.

Fans and writers have seen this situation develop both before and since. They often ask if there is a temptation to ease up a bit, hoping to lose a few games near the end of the season and finish behind another team to ensure getting an important draft choice.

I can say that I never considered "letting up," which is only a euphemism for "losing on purpose." I went into every game thinking *win* with my customary intensity. Playing to win was such an ingrained habit that it would have been difficult, if not impossible, for me to do what was necessary to lose.

Not that it would be impossible for a coach to ease off and increase his chance of losing. A few strategic substitutions late in a close game might almost guarantee a loss without being obvious to the fans. If writers asked about a substitution, the coach could even give an answer that has a certain logic: "We can't make the playoffs. I've got to think about next year, and the only way I can find out who I want to keep is to play everyone."

Then the coach could rationalize his behavior to himself by considering his obligation to the team owner, who is paying him to put people in the seats. With the right draft choice, the team will win more games the following season and increase attendance. The fans might have to sit through a few seemingly meaningless losses at the tail end of a season, but the next year they would see a better team. Even the players would profit—the new draftee could mean playoff money to them.

However persuasive such thinking may seem, to me it was always pure crap. The coach would have to look at himself in the mirror every morning and realize that he had done something that was morally, professionally and legally wrong. He was using an end—winning next year —to justify a means—losing on purpose this year.

And there are also practical problems. I am certain that most players would see through the substituting and realize what the coach was up to. How could the coach even claim to be building a winning attitude when the players can see he's willing to lose?

We won five of our last ten games and finished with

thirty-six wins and forty-six losses. The Celtics won thirty-four and lost forty-eight. They would pick fourth in the draft and we would pick fifth. If this meant we would lose Cowens, that's the way it would have to be. Losing games on purpose was too high a price to pay.

I still thought that we might get Cowens. From everything we heard—and NBA general managers are on the phone talking every day during drafting time—he might still be available when our turn came.

The draft would be held on a telephone conference hookup. Joe and I sat before microphones in the Cincinnati Gardens Booster Club. To get as much publicity as possible, we had invited the TV-news cameras and the public to come and watch.

Just before the drafting began, Joe turned to me and said, "If Lacey and Cowens are both gone, Cooz, who do we pick?"

"You've got the mike," I said. "You pick."

I wasn't kidding. After Lacey and Cowens, the only players we had considered were Geoff Petrie and John Hummer, but in our opinion they were not worth the money we would have to pay them as first-round picks. With the ABA competing for talent, a first-round choice could demand and get $100,000 a year for three years with a no-cut clause. Or more. If the kid flopped you could have half a million dollars sitting on your bench and doing nothing for three years.

The wise move for us, if we couldn't get Lacey or Cowens, would have been to say "pass" on the first round and then pick the best talent still available in the second. But we couldn't do that, either. The press and the fans would have jumped all over us for passing up the top choices.

The drafting began. As expected, Detroit picked Bob Lanier. San Diego went second and took Rudy Tomjanovich, apparently unable or unwilling to pay what the glamor boy of the draft, Pete Maravich, would be asking. Atlanta had obtained San Francisco's first-round pick and the Hawks took Maravich.

Now it was Boston's turn.

"Dave Cowens," I heard Arnold say over the hookup, and I guess my heart dropped a little. But at least now I knew we would get the other big center we wanted. Joe said, "Sam Lacey."

Lacey, after a slow start, has turned out to be a better-than-average NBA center, making the Western Division All-Star team in 1975. Cowens developed into the second-best center in the league, was the NBA's Most Valuable Player in 1973 and helped the Celtics win the championship in 1974.

Although Cowens was a "sleeper" to many fans, he was no secret to pro scouts. Over the next few seasons, as I watched him develop into a superstar, I consoled myself with the thought that I had been beaten to Cowens by a man with a great eye for talent. *Arnold saw in Cowens what I saw in him,* I told myself. *So I should have known he would pick him.*

About three years after that draft, I was playing tennis with a good friend and former Celtic teammate, Ernie Barrett. Ernie was then the athletic director at Kansas State University. After the match, while we were relaxing, Ernie mentioned Sam Lacey. "You know," he said, "I never thought Lacey would be an NBA center. You really have been fortunate that he's worked out so well for you."

I said that Sam had worked very hard.

"You know," Ernie continued, leaning back in a chair, "I remember the day before you drafted Lacey. I was sitting in my office and I got a telephone call from Arnold. He asked me what I thought of Lacey because he said he was thinking of drafting him."

I sat up straight.

"Yeah," Ernie went on, "but I think I talked him out of it. I told Arnold I didn't think there was any chance that Lacey could play in the NBA. I guess maybe Arnold listened to me and that's why he drafted Cowens instead."

Until Ernie reads this, he will never know how close I came to knocking him off that chair.

# THE
# BLACK
# ATHLETE

After we had picked Sam Lacey in the opening round of the 1970 draft, we got the second choice in the second round. This was our payment from San Francisco for Odie Smith. We chose a six-foot guard from the University of Texas at El Paso. His name was Nate Archibald.

About a month earlier, when I knew that Oscar would be leaving, I had told Draff Young, who was on the road scouting college talent, what to look for.

"I'd like to get a playmaking guard," I said, "someone who can quarterback our offense. He doesn't have to be a scorer. I want someone who can penetrate defenses and is emotionally and mentally able to run a team."

Most fans don't realize how difficult it is to find that kind of a player. If I had to do it over again and rebuild a team, I would value the ball-handling guard higher than anyone except perhaps a Jabbar or a Chamberlain.

Scoring guards are a dime a dozen. Guards who know the game and can dribble and pass are scarce, as I had discovered at BC. If I had a talented six-foot-one son, I'd tell him to work hard on his dribbling, passing and knowledge of basketball. If he can handle the ball and think the game, even if he isn't a great shooter, he's going to make the college and pro scouts sit up.

A few weeks after our conversation, Draff came back and told me he thought he'd found the ball-handling guard I wanted. "His name is Archibald," Draff said. "He's averaging only about twelve or fourteen points a game but he plays for a well-disciplined, ball-control offense. He's the one who brings the ball over for them."

Shortly after the draft, Joe and I sat down with Sam Lacey and his attorneys. We knew we were going to have to pay a lot of money and we were right. After much negotiating we signed Sam for about $600,000 over five years.

We didn't give as much thought to signing Archibald, our second-round choice. We knew that most unknown second-round picks could be signed easily. We thought Archibald would accept $75,000 to $100,000 for three years. the first-round picks get the bulk of the money because the talent to play in the pros is so rare. Usually no more than twenty college seniors can make the jump to the NBA and ABA each year, and since everyone is scouting this talent intensively, most of it is gone by the first round. After that almost everyone else is a sleeper. Players picked in the third round or below, we were discovering, were often handed an offer and told to take it or leave it.

Archibald's team had gone to no major tournaments, and as a result Tiny—as he was called at El Paso—had received little exposure. In fact, neither Joe nor I had ever seen him play—nor had we met him. Then he was invited to play in an All-Star game in Memphis. Joe and I went down to talk to him.

We checked in at the hotel where he was staying. A few hours before the game, we phoned and invited him to come up to say hello. He came in looking extremely shy and nervous. I shook hands with him.

"I'm Bob Cousy," I said, "and this is our general manager, Joe Axelson. We're very happy to have you with us."

He mumbled something and sat down in a chair. I could tell that he wished he were somewhere else. Suddenly he reminded me of a twenty-two-year-old kid from Holy Cross who had felt the same way twenty years earlier when he first met Arnold Auerbach.

"Have you got an agent?" Joe asked him.

"No. But I've got a friend in New York who may represent me."

"Okay. We'd rather deal with you when you have representation. After this game tonight, aren't you going to be playing in that All-Star game in Indianapolis on Sunday?"

"Yes, sir."

Joe said he would try to arrange for Tiny and his agent to fly from Indianapolis to Cincinnati after that game to negotiate a contract.

We chatted for a few more minutes, Joe and I doing most of the talking. Archibald left looking as shy and scared as when he had entered. If we had put a contract in front of him then and there, we would probably have signed him for $100,000 over three years. As it turned out, we would have saved the Royals a hell of a lot of money.

That evening, watching Tiny play for the first time, I

saw that he was everything that I had sent Draff to find: the quick, fast guard who knew how to handle the ball and penetrate defenses. But I also saw something I hadn't expected: he could score. He threw in something like twenty-eight points.

Joe and I left the arena in a thoughtful mood. "You know," I said as we walked back to the hotel, "we may have gotten something extra with this kid. He may be a fairly good shooter."

A few days later, Tiny played in Indianapolis. The game was shown on national TV. Tiny scored somewhere around thirty-eight points and was the game's outstanding player. Suddenly, fans in Cincinnati were talking about him.

In Hawaii the promoters of another All-Star tournament had seen the Indianapolis game on TV. They phoned Tiny and invited him to fly to the islands for their tournament. Instead of coming to Cincinnati, as Joe had arranged, Tiny flew to Hawaii.

There he scored 122 points in three games. In the last game he scored 51. Joe and I happened to be talking to Tiny's college coach, Don Haskins, at his office in El Paso when the results came in. "I'm just as surprised as you guys," Don said. "He played for me for three years and I never knew he could score like that."

About a week later, Tiny walked into our office in Cincinnati with his agents. Everyone expected us to sign him, whatever the cost. There's a saying in the NBA that when you're trying to sign a draft choice like this, you wait until the agent is finished asking and then you say, "Fine, and is there anything else you want?"

We signed Tiny for something like $465,000 over three

years. In a couple of weeks and a few All-Star games, Tiny had made himself almost $400,000.

Several times during the summer I flew to Cincinnati to make promotional appearances. But by now I was beginning to question seriously whether the NBA had a future in Cincinnati. One reason was some of the letters I was getting. They were always unsigned and they said, "Who the hell wants to go to your games and watch those niggers run up and down the court?"

My reaction to the bigots, although I never said it publicly, was, "You haven't seen anything yet." I was visualizing a starting team of Norm Van Lier and Flynn Robinson in the backcourt, Sam Lacey at center, and Johnny Green and Tom Van Arsdale in the corners. Four of the five were black. And on the bench, my top four substitutes, Tiny Archibald, Charlie Paulk, Fred Foster and Bill Turner, were black, too.

Bill Russell used to claim that there was a quota system in the NBA, that a gentlemen's agreement limited the number of blacks on any one team. To me this has always been a lot of crap. I worked closely with the front office, and the racial composition of the team came up only rarely. In discussion of a trade, for instance, someone would say, "That gives us nine out of twelve."

But everyone's first concern was to win. You did what was necessary to get the best basketball players, and more often than not the best players were black.

In the 1950's I had played with the first black to reach the NBA—Chuck Cooper. By now, twenty years later, almost 70 percent of the players in the league were black, and it seemed the percentage might go higher.

Most basketball coaches will tell you that if you match two players of the same height, one black and one white, the black player will outjump his opponent more often than not. The superiority of black basketball players has become a cliché. When coaches get together, one is sure to say, "I've got the one black kid in this country who can't jump."

Most black athletes are loose, agile, mobile, quick and have jumping ability—all the things a coach looks for in a basketball player. These are blessings they are born with. Of course, white athletes are also born with these blessings. But it has been my observation that perhaps three out of a hundred black kids have great athletic talent while only one or two of a hundred white kids have it. Again the general impression is borne out by a shopworn saying. When coaches see a white boy who can jump or who moves with extraordinary quickness, they say, "He should have been born black, he's that good."

And more black athletes have the hunger to excel in sports. Most white kids have more options and distractions. There's less drive to go up there and get that ball. They aren't as apt to develop their athletic skills as black kids. We saw earlier that very few players, black or white, make it into professional sports. One of the requirements for making it is that deep hunger to excel and improve yourself. I had it as a youngster, and as a coach I recognized it in more black players than white.

Not all coaches appreciated the black athletes. Some insisted that blacks tended to be lazy, didn't hustle, were less coachable, couldn't play a team game and folded under pressure because they didn't think fast enough.

Having played in the NBA with or against people like

Oscar, Elgin Baylor, Bill Russell and others, I had reason to doubt such "wisdom." At Boston College, John Austin had shown me that the bigots were wrong in every way.

As for the business of not thinking well under pressure, I thought people who brought up that argument showed a real lack of understanding. Basketball is an instinctive game. In pressure situations you don't have time to think —you must act or react instantly. If we needed two points to win at BC, we gave the ball to John Austin. At Cincinnati we gave it to Oscar or (later) to Tiny. These were the men who played best under pressure. I always said I would rather have a player with an IQ of 85—black or white—who has an instinctive sense for the game than a player with an IQ of 140 who doesn't.

At Cincinnati, for the first time, I was part of a team where the majority of the players were black. I soon came to believe it is a mistake to assume that there is a "black personality" as opposed to a "white personality."

We are all products of our environment, our traits determined by experiences and our reactions to them as we mature. One of these experiences, obviously, is being a member of a black minority in a white world. But that, it seemed to me, was one experience out of many. And many other experiences are common to the growing-up process whether you are white or black.

A man like Oscar, for example, might carry a chip on his shoulder and reject authority because of something white men or white society did to him. A white kid may carry a chip on his shoulder because of something Daddy did to him. Practically speaking, they have the same personality—both reject authority—although the causes are different.

Norm Van Lier was a very proud person. One night, as he was leaving a bar in Cincinnati, he heard three long-shoremen make some kind of racial remark. All by himself he wiped out the three of them.

If he had been white and one-legged and those long-shoremen had abused him for being one-legged or white, Norm would have fought them just the same. He would not let anyone abuse him, not because he was white, black or one-legged, but because he was a very proud person. And he was not proud and militant because it just happened it was fashionable right then for young blacks to be that way. He would have been as proud and militant on the first slave ship—or in the first labor movement, or whatever.

Norm was also about the only young player I coached who had so much confidence in himself that he could walk into a huddle after messing up a play and say, "Sorry, that was my fault."

Most young players in the pros are not that way, perhaps because they were pampered blue-chippers for so long, or because they are now making so much money it frightens them.

A few years later, after Norm had left the team, all five of my players were screaming at each other during a time-out. One was blaming another for this or that. Another was complaining about the officials. Everything was wrong except themselves. They had every excuse in the book.

I blew up. "You know," I said, "I've had only one guy in three years of coaching here who ever came back during a time-out and said, 'I did something wrong' instead of

'Why didn't you catch that pass?' or 'Why didn't you see that I was open?' "

That was Norman. If I had been black, I always thought I would have been like him: the young militant, demonstrating, standing up and demanding to be treated the same way whether I was white or black.

At the other end of the pole was Sam Lacey. I found that I had to light a fire under Sam to get him up for a game. Part of the reason for his lack of aggressiveness and confidence could be traced back to growing up in a small town in Mississippi. Coming into the high-paid and pressure-filled world of pro basketball might scare anyone. But coming from a climate of black subjugation, Sam was more frightened than most. When you're frightened, you don't communicate well and you don't learn very quickly. Sam's fright, I think, slowed his education as a player. I have also wondered whether I went too hard on him sometimes, taking too much for granted and intensifying his problem.

Once, after he had been with us for two or three years, I shouted at him during practice, "To the weak side, Sam, go to the weak side."

Sam immediately ran to the strong side of the court.

Draff Young was standing next to me. "Maybe," Draff said, "he doesn't know what weak side means."

I couldn't believe that. The weak side of the court is the side where the ball isn't; the strong side is where the ball is. A basketball player should know that as instinctively as a soldier on a drill field knows his left from his right.

I called Sam over to where we were standing. "Sam," I asked, "what does weak side mean?"

He looked at the floor. "I don't know," he said.

Gently, I explained it to him. Later I thought of how Sam had sat for so long, hearing me talk about weak side, yet not knowing what I was talking about. In some of those plays he was the hub of our offense. I began to understand even better why he often looked frightened out there.

Tiny Archibald came to the NBA frightened, but Tiny also came with the street smarts of a kid from the big-city ghetto and he learned much more quickly than Sam. Because our backgrounds were so similar—we both came from poor sections of the same city—I empathized more with him than with any of the other players, black or white. I could project what it must have been like for this shy, reticent kid to leave the black ghetto for a white man's college in Texas. I had been terrified just going from Queens to Holy Cross. His college life must have been more difficult than mine, but again I could feel what he was feeling when he had to speak at a banquet or meet strangers. I had been nearly as shy and fearful.

Watching Tiny develop in a short time from a little-known college player to an NBA superstar, I began to notice the strong forces that could pull a young black athlete apart.

On one hand, he has been told, "Whitey is just using you. He'll get rid of you when he can't use you any longer. Get everything you can now." He knows of black athletes who have been ripped off by colleges or had their careers blighted in the pros by a bigoted coach or general manager.

On the other hand, the athlete's white coach and general manager seem to treat him with respect and affection. He is given almost anything he wants: a college education, a $100,000-a-year salary. Through sports he has met whites who have been genuinely good to him and he has developed a fondness for them. If he is a superstar, the question he hears most often is, "What else do you want?"

So the young man is torn in two directions: one by his suspicion of his white bosses, the other by the loyalty he feels to the men who are giving him affection as well as material things. The player may be only twenty-two or twenty-three years old, but if he can't handle these contrary emotions he will be confused, guilt-ridden and unhappy. Even if he is being treated with respect, he may do and say some silly things. And if he *is* being callously used by his team, he will soon learn to use other people the same way.

Although there may be racial tensions in pro teams, in my experience they remain below the surface. In all my years with the Celtics I was not aware of any real antagonism, nor did I see any as a coach.

It is true that on many pro teams black and white players do not spend much time together off the court. A common pattern on the road is for a few of the white players to go off to a movie. The black players congregate in someone's room to listen to music and entertain themselves. Among themselves the black players laugh more and sharpen their humor, often on each other. Perhaps this is a way to release some of the tension they feel living in a white man's world. Whatever the reason, pro basketball is richer for the black sense of humor. Some of my happiest memories of Celtics days are of moments when K.C. Jones or Satch Sanders would make a crack and Bill Russell's laughter would echo through the halls.

It was always my belief as a player—and my coaching experiences tended to confirm it—that a baseball team is more likely to be split by racial emotions than a basketball or a football team. In baseball each player is pretty much on his own whether he is at bat, pitching, or trying to catch a ball. In basketball and football you depend on other people to block for you, tackle for you, pass to you, rebound for you, get the ball to you. If you're going to be successful, you need the help of the other guy. And that dependence, I always thought, diluted any bigotry that a player might bring to a team.

The competitive urge manifests itself in people in a lot of bad ways, I suppose, but that same urge is also the reason for often bringing us together in teamwork.

# ROAD
# TRIP

That summer of 1970 I spent most of July and August at the camp in New Hampshire, getting reacquainted with Marie, who had been at college in Boston. In the fall she would be a sophomore, and next year Tish would be ready for college, too.

But in early September, Missie, Tish and I flew back to Cincinnati for my second season with the Royals. We rented the same apartment. "I like Cincinnati," Missie told me, "but I'm from the East and if you're going to move me to the Midwest you might as well move me to Peking. I feel that far away from home."

She knew few people here. "The only people I know," she once told me, "are the butcher and the mailman, and I can't stand the mailman."

At Celtic games she had always enjoyed socializing with the wives of the players, even after I had retired. But here she had to sit apart from the wives. "I know what the Celtic wives used to say about Auerbach when Bob was playing," she told people. "And I don't want to hear what the Royals wives are saying about Bob."

I told reporters that I saw progress on the floor. But I knew we had a long way to go.

"How long do you think it will take to win a championship?" I was asked.

"Twenty years," I'd say, and I wasn't altogether kidding. It had taken New York, the NBA champions of the previous season, more than twenty years to win a championship, and New York was the richest franchise in the league. In the past twelve years only four teams had won the NBA title, and three of those teams had guys named Russell, Chamberlain and Jabbar. The fourth had Willis Reed and surrounded him with a lot of high-priced talent. So all I had to do to break into this charmed circle was either be lucky enough to draft a Russell, Chamberlain or Jabbar—only three of whom had come along in the past fifteen years—or spend enough of Max Jacobs' money to surround Sam Lacey with a lot of high-priced talent.

We lost our first five games, won three in a row, then went through stretches where we lost six of seven, and seven in a row. There were consolations. Tiny Archibald was showing us not only that he could be a starter in his rookie year, but that he could one day be a superstar. Sam Lacey began very slowly, but I knew that centers develop slowly and that Sam could one day be a strong player at his position. John Green was giving us another excellent year. And Norm Van Lier, by giving a little extra, often made the rest of the team play a little over its head.

But I still had the problems of losing. And I still had a competitive spirit that didn't like getting its face rubbed into the mud night after night. Winning magnifies pressure, but losing, I was discovering, magnifies problems.

*Cincinnati, Feb. 6, 1971*—I awake in our apartment at a little past seven in the morning. I arrived home at around two in the morning after flying in from Boston. It is an idiosyncracy of mine that no matter what time I go to bed, I generally arise around seven.

We lost last night in Boston. Our won-lost record is now 24–33 about two-thirds of the way through this 1970–71 season. Tonight we will play Philadelphia at home. Right after the game we will fly to Atlanta for a game tomorrow night against the Hawks. We will be on the road for all of the next two weeks.

While I am away, Missie will drive back to Worcester in our car to visit her sister and our daughter Marie. She has been making these commuting trips fairly often when I go on longer road trips. I tell her I worry about her being alone in that big house.

Around noon I go to the office. I answer some correspondence and read reports from Draff about college players he's been seeing on the road. I take from a cabinet a file folder labeled "Philadelphia," containing reports I've written to myself after each game we've played against the 76ers. These reports will provide the basis of what I tell the players before the game when we go over defensive and offensive assignments.

At five-thirty I drive to the arena. In the dressing room, trainer Joe Keefe is standing in front of the rubbing table, taping players' ankles. Like most NBA trainers, Joe doubles as traveling secretary. He checks with the airlines on changes in flight times and arranges for chartered buses to take us from airports to hotels, from hotels to arenas, and back again. This trip, we will see eight cities in the next thirteen days.

I talk briefly with Joe about assorted injuries. Around us the players sit on stools, undressing. Norm Van Lier's tape recorder is sending out soul music and I have to raise my voice so Joe can hear me. I always liked a quiet dressing room when I played. The quiet helped to tighten me and get me up for competition. But if music gets these kids up, fine. I only asked that the music be turned off just before the game time so I could go over assignments and be heard.

We lose to Philadelphia, 118–109. There is quiet in the bus as it rolls through the night to the Cincinnati airport. I am seated in the front with a newspaperman, Barry McDermott, our radio broadcaster, Dom Valentino, and trainer Joe Keefe. Most of the players have migrated to the rear of the bus, where they are talking in low tones among themselves. If we had won, the bus would be reverberating with loud talk, laughter and music.

*Atlanta, Feb.* 7—We didn't get into our motel until three or four in the morning. Most of us stuck to our rooms until it was time for the bus to take us to the arena late in the afternoon for the game. We play a strong game, come close, but lose our third straight, 121–118.

*Seattle, Feb.* 9—Finally, we have some spare time; we will be staying three nights. Today and tomorrow we're off, and the next night we play.

In the plane on the way here I called Tommy Van Arsdale, our captain, over to my seat and told him, "Twelve-thirty curfew tonight, Tommy. Pass the word."

On the subject of checking on the players, Arnold had always said, "You can't be a policeman." I agreed. As a coach I believed that you can destroy your relationship with your players by making them toe the line to a lot of chicken rules. Pro players want to be treated like men—even though some of them are about as sophisticated as ten-year-old boys.

Most players are aware that the guy who burns the candles at both ends just isn't going to function on a basketball court for very long. When I found a guy who wasn't aware of that reality, I tried to teach him the facts of NBA life: "If you can get a lady to say yes before one o'clock in the morning, I couldn't care less. The physical act doesn't affect you one way or other. But when you can't get her to say yes until you've sat up with her until four in the morning, it won't be the lady or the yes that will hurt you, it's the staying out until four in the morning."

*Seattle, Feb. 11*—The SuperSonics hang a fourth straight defeat on us, 119–101.

*San Francisco, Feb. 12*—On the flight from Seattle we run into some turbulence. Sam Lacey suddenly lets out a long, piercing wail and shields his head under his arms. The other passengers in the first-class cabin almost leap out of their seats. The sound is absolutely eerie. But we are getting accustomed to this reaction from Sam. He does not like flying and even the slightest dip in the plane will draw that wail out of him.

I spend the afternoon in my hotel room writing a report on last night's game for my files. Perhaps I should write it immediately after the game, when my impressions are fresher, but I am usually too exhausted.

Tonight we lose our fifth straight, the Warriors beating us, 133–119.


*San Diego, Feb. 13*—Some of the players are having trouble remembering what city we're in, since this is the fourth strange town this week. But as our bus speeds down the freeway toward our motel, everyone knows we are in San Diego. The motel is in the middle of nowhere.

I have a team rule against the players' drinking at the bar of the hotel where we are staying. It simply doesn't look good for the players to come back to the hotel, especially after a loss, throw down their bags and run for the bar. As Arnold once told me, "If the newspapermen are looking for a reason why you've been losing, you may be handing them a reason that won't be true but will be embarrassing."

Not that drinking is a problem on this team; nor is it on any NBA team, in my experience, except for a few isolated cases. Still, the typical basketball player likes to go out and have a couple of beers to release the pressure after a game.

Here in San Diego, where there is no bar nearby, I let the players drink at the motel bar if they ask permission. In the afternoon Tom Van Arsdale says he is having some friends come by after the game and asks if he can drink with them. I say yes, but not very cheerfully. A little later it occurs to me that I would have said yes with a smile if we had been winning. But when you're losing you can get surly over being asked for the smallest favors.

I am even unhappier back in my room that night. We have lost our sixth straight, San Diego beating us, 120–116.

*Los Angeles, Feb. 14*—I spend the day writing my report on yesterday's game and reading a book I've brought along. Later, I go over the file folder I've brought along on the Lakers. I nibble at lunch. I won't eat again until after the game. When I do, I have very little appetite. We have lost number seven in a row.

*Eugene, Oregon, Feb. 15*—This is our first off-day in the past five. Coming up on the plane this morning from Los Angeles, some of the players were kidding with the stewardesses. There was a lot of laughing. Sitting in front and reading, I thought, *If some of you guys would spend less time fooling around with the stewardesses and making jokes, maybe we would win a game.*

Seven straight losses and the pressure is building.

After we get to our hotel, I see very little of the players. Nearly all of them stick to their rooms, watching television and ordering food from room service—at least during daylight hours.

The relationship between the pro coach and player is cursory. As a college coach I would invite kids to come to my office to talk to them about their classroom work. That almost always led to any other problems they might be having, with their girl friends, with their parents, or whatever. My interest, of course, wasn't completely altruistic. I wanted to know, and get rid of, any problems that might draw the kid's attention away from playing basketball.

As a pro coach, on the other hand, I rarely talk to the players about anything except basketball. And when they do come around, most often they want a special favor. One player wanted to be met at the airport at the end of a road trip by a chauffeured limousine, because his wife couldn't pick him up. We laughed about this request, but this kind of attitude was irritating after a while.

In the afternoon, while I am reading in my room, there is a knock at the door. I open it. Outside there is a delegation of four or five players.

"Coach," one of them says, "can we extend the curfew until one-thirty tonight?"

I say no, rather curtly, and close the door. Their request rubs me the wrong way.

I know that if we had been winning I would have said yes. But now I find myself angry that losing doesn't seem to bother them the way it bothers me. Instead of being concerned about some new favor, why aren't they getting together and trying to figure out why they've lost seven straight?

We'd have been more likely to do that when I was with the Celtics. We were a winning team, and losing never became a familiar, everyday occurrence. But player attitudes have changed a lot, too. Generally speaking, the pro athlete of today is much more concerned with his own world, his own personal goals, his own immediate financial success, than he is with the success of his team.

Sure, he wants the team to win. But he's not willing to run as hard or as long to make sure that it does win. And he keeps his eye on his own statistics, knowing that a fat scoring or rebounding average will be a valuable weapon when he negotiates his next contract. Self-interest too often becomes selfishness and the game suffers. The change in athletes should hardly be a surprise, I guess. In 1946, when I was an All–New York City high school player, I got exactly two offers of college scholarships. Today an All-City player would get two hundred or more offers. From the time he is fourteen or fifteen, he is buttered up by college recruiters and big-name coaches. In many colleges he is given almost anything he demands.

Then an agent comes along, begging the player to let him do the negotiating with a pro team. No doubt a good agent is a necessity for today's pro athletes. But many of these agents' arrangements are so all-inclusive that the agents literally run the athletes' lives.

I once overheard one of our players talking by phone with his agent halfway across the country. "I've got a parking ticket," he said. "What should I do with it?"

The agent said to send the ticket to him.

In this kind of arrangement, an athlete sends all his bills to the agent, and the agent takes care of all the player's problems—from a parking ticket to divorcing his wife. I can see this athlete retiring from the sport as a near millionaire in his early thirties. Yet he has never done anything much more complicated than putting a stamp on an envelope and mailing it to his agent. I wonder how well equipped he is going to be to take care of his money, his family and himself, especially if someone comes along and decides to hustle him out of some cash.

We have a notion that participation in athletics helps a person develop and mature. This may be true for the average athlete, who plays hard and likes to win but doesn't have the talent to reach the top. But it's not nearly as true for today's blue-chippers and pro stars. Too often they have been shielded from having to make hard decisions by the recruiters, coaches and agents. They are pampered and spoiled.

*Eugene, Oregon, Feb. 16*—Thank God, we snap the losing streak. We beat the Trail Blazers, 109–102.

After the game I have an appetite for the first time since we began this long road trip almost two weeks ago. I go out for a late dinner with the newspaperman who is with us. Losing, I have discovered, diminishes all your appetites but winning heightens them.

I go back to my room. I look in a mirror and take a deep breath, and I think, *Hey, a win, this is what it's all about.*

I have a sense of euphoria. It seems to me that this must be the way it is for a heroin addict. But I know that soon this high will level off, and I'll crave another. The next high for me will be the next good win.

# THE MIND
# OF A
# COACH

**C**leveland, *Feb. 19*—This is the last stop of the trip. After that victory over Portland in Eugene, we went to Phoenix and lost. We have lost eight of our last nine games. But we are still in second place in our division, a half-game ahead of Atlanta.

At a little after six, I walk from the hotel to the Cleveland Arena. I stay away from the players until a few minutes before game time.

When I come in, someone switches off the music. I stand in the middle of the small, rectangular room. Pants and overcoats are draped on hooks on the walls. The players are sitting, bony knees facing me, on stools and collapsible chairs. A toilet flushes to my left. A player hurries out, sits down.

I tell them that they know this Cleveland team so I am not going to give them any long review. Most of the Cleveland players can shoot. But in the past we have been able to rattle them when we played aggressive defense.

I start Van Lier, Flynn Robinson, Sam Lacey, Greg Hyder (a rookie forward who was our third-round draft choice) and Tom Van Arsdale. Of their players, forward Johnny Johnson is their best. Walt Wesley (a former Royal) is at center.

From the start we are running, pushing the ball quickly upcourt. We know from the past that if we run against Cleveland, we can usually turn up enough lay-ups and short jumpers to beat them. On defense, however, we are playing passively—just what we can't afford to do. The Cavaliers run their patterns, set screens and shoot well.

One of the referees is Jake O'Donnell. I used to like Jake to work our games. I thought he was very fair. But then during a game against Philadelphia, Jake blew a rule by letting a 76er leave the game before a jump ball and then return later.

Jake said yes. He simply blew the rule; everyone, including referees, makes mistakes. Later in the game, when Ramsay sent the player back, I complained to Jake but he let the player stay in—I guess because he had already told Ramsay it would be all right.

We lost and after the game we submitted a protest, claiming that Philadelphia had used an ineligible player. Commissioner Walter Kennedy said he would take the protest under advisement and issue a ruling at the end of the season if the game affected either team's getting into the playoffs. As it turned out, the game had no effect on the playoffs and Kennedy never made a ruling.

I got the feeling that Jake thought we should have said nothing and taken our lumps without protesting. After that game, we lost something like thirteen or fourteen straight when Jake was one of the officials. I know you look for excuses when you're losing, but still we didn't think Jake was being completely fair to us. Occasionally, when Jake would call something against us, I would needle him about that Philadelphia decision. Some of my comments cost me technical fouls, which meant a fine for me from the league.

In this game Jake calls a foul against Sam Lacey. I jump to my feet, but I keep my mouth shut. Lacey wasn't anywhere near the man he was supposed to have fouled and that's one of Sam's problems. He has to stick closer to Wesley, pressuring him so that Wesley can't get into position to catch the ball near the basket—"low," in the parlance of the business. Once you let an NBA center get the ball in low, chances are that you will be burned. Wesley got the ball in low, went up for a fall-away jumper and scored. According to Jake, Lacey fouled Wesley on the shot. It costs us three points.

A little later, I call a time-out. "Sam," I say, "you've got to put pressure on your man. You can't let him have that position."

I have been saying this all season and Sam still allows people to take positions on him. It's hard, physical work to stop them from taking those positions and I know by now that I have got to keep on top of Sam to get him to work that hard.

I talk to the other players. It's a truism of this profession that you have to treat each player differently—and this is especially true when you're telling them what they're doing wrong. With one guy, you have to precede your criticism with encouragement. With another, if you even look at him sideways he may go off and sulk. Another is so high-strung that you have to tone him down instead of trying to stimulate him. Still another player may need to be stepped on.

One day, I sometimes tell myself, a coach will have a psychiatrist instead of a trainer sitting on the bench next to him.

They lead, 37–28, at the end of the first period. I begin to make substitutions. Here again, the coach must be a psychologist. Some substitutions are made because of obvious factors—the score, the need to match the size or speed of someone on the other side. But other substitutions are for more subtle reasons. One of your players may play particularly well in this building or an opposing player may lose his cool when you play a certain player against him.

I notice that Tiny is taking the quick shot—the first one that opens up for him. And I know why: that Cleveland guard, Joe Cooke, is crawling into Tiny's armpits, he's guarding him that closely. Tiny takes this kind of defensive pressure personally, as though it's an affront to his manhood. He wants to destroy this guy and do it all by himself. He will take the quick shot whenever he gets the ball, rather than be patient.

During a time-out I tell him, "Keep your cool, wait for the better shot. It's a long game. That defense is going to wear down."

There are about four minutes to go in the half. We're reducing their lead but I'm not too happy about the way we've been getting most of our hoops—many of them on outside shooting by Van Arsdale and Robinson. We're in trouble if we have to try to stay even with Cleveland by shooting from the outside. They're the better-shooting team to begin with, and they have the mental advantage of shooting in their own arena.

They lead at the half, 57–54. I decide I will make a speech during the half-time intermission.

I tell them that they played very well during the second period. I remind them about keeping up an aggressive defense and controlling the boards. Then I concede that this has not been the best of road trips.

"I know things are going bad," I say, "our bad games are behind us. It's time for things to turn in our favor. We're still in the playoff picture, as bad as we've been going. Let's not get discouraged. Let's be ready when things turn our way. Stick to our basic things—aggressive defense, board control, the fast break—and we can go out of here with a big win."

In the third quarter Cleveland begins to look in to six-foot-eleven Wesley when they bring down the ball. By now Wesley has scored about twenty points and they are obviously hoping he has the hot hand.

Again, during a time-out, I tell Sam to keep Wesley from getting the ball low. I tell him to overplay Wesley by getting in front of him "half a man."

For a while Sam overplays Wesley, cutting him off from the ball. Cleveland goes back to its usual outside-shooting game, and their shots are not hitting as often. Sam is coming down with good rebounds, and we turn up a couple of fast breaks. Van Arsdale and Flynn Robinson are hitting from the outside. They increase their lead, but we are still in the game. Early in the final period we are behind, 93–82.

They go back to pouring their offense in to Wesley. And Sam stops working hard. He stands behind Wesley, no longer keeping him from getting the ball in low. With the score 95–86, Wesley gets the ball low, turns for a shot, and as he lets it go he is fouled by Sam. The shot goes in, Wesley completes the three-point play and they lead, 98–86.

The rest of the way is garbage time. Wesley—perhaps a twenty-point scorer at best—has the hot hand now. He scores fifty points before the night is over.

I had already been vocal about some calls by Jake O'Donnell. Several times I reminded him loudly about that Philadelphia decision: "Jake, just for the record, you're not fooling anybody. I know what that call was really all about."

He ignores me and I don't get hit with a technical. Not that it would make any difference, either his decision or any technical he might have called against me. Games are seldom won or lost on official calls. We lose, 125–109.

That night we board a plane to go home to Cincinnati after twelve straight days on the road. We have only one win in our last ten games. The players are quiet behind me in the dark plane. I am looking forward to seeing Missie and Tish again, but for most of the trip I am thinking, *Maybe I should have done this . . . Maybe I should have done that . . .*

# NOT
# MAKING
# IT

**W**e finished with a 33–49 record in 1970–71, my second season at Cincinnati. We would be picking fourth in the spring-of-1971 draft.

Cleveland, picking first, told us they would probably take either Notre Dame's Austin Carr or UCLA's Sidney Wicks. Portland was picking second, and they told us they would go for whichever of the two was still available.

Buffalo was picking third, ahead of us. We called Buffalo general manager Eddie Donovan.

"I like Kenny Durrett," Eddie told us.

So did we. Everyone we had talked to had told us that Durrett, a willowy forward from LaSalle, was in a class with Wicks and Carr. Donovan was also considering Elmore Smith, a Kentucky State center.

We were not interested in Smith. We knew he was asking two and a half million dollars for three years, and we thought Lacey was at least as good and probably better.

We began to think about a strategy that might influence Buffalo to pick Smith and leave us Durrett. Joe got on the phone and talked to nearly every general manager in the league. "We think a lot of Elmore Smith," he told each of them. "We're thinking very seriously of drafting him."

We wanted everyone in the league grapevine to be talking Smith. Sure enough, within a few hours, we were getting calls from other clubs: "Hey, what do you hear about this kid Smith?"

A couple of days later the draft began. Cleveland picked Austin Carr. Portland picked Sidney Wicks.

It was Buffalo's turn. Eddie Donovan came on the hookup and said, "Elmore Smith."

Joe and I sat back and smiled. Our turn. Joe said, "Kenny Durrett."

I doubt that our touting of Elmore Smith swayed Eddie Donovan into picking him—but it might have helped. I don't know what we would have done if Eddie had picked Durrett. We didn't want Elmore Smith. And behind Smith there was no one we thought could help us. None of the others drafted in the first round became stars, and some of them didn't make it at all in the NBA.

Identifying and acquiring pro basketball talent is much more difficult, in my opinion, than identifying big league baseball or pro football talent—with two exceptions. The exceptions are the baseball pitcher and the football quarterback, two jobs which also require a rare combination of skills. When you consider how few young players become big-league pitchers or pro quarterbacks at the outset, you can understand why so few All-Americas become ABA or NBA starters right away.

What is even more frustrating is that when you do manage to acquire a guy with this rare talent, plus the willingness to work to improve that talent, he still may not be able to do the job for you—for reasons that can often be mysterious. We were about to discover this with Kenny Durrett.

We signed Kenny for 1.4 million dollars for five years, and we figured we had gotten him cheaply. Smith, Wicks and Carr each signed for two million or more. But unluckily, Kenny wasn't a bargain.

He had twisted a knee during his senior year in college. He continued to play, and his doctors assured us that there was no problem. Unfortunately, there was a problem. He came to pre-season training in 1971 and started the season with us. But the knee got worse and had to be operated on. Then in 1972 the same thing happened all over again. He played very little for us.

At training camp in his third season, he won a job as a starting forward. He was a leaper and had great moves. He had speed and quickness, and an instinct for the game. He was not a pure shooter but he knew where the basket was and he could put the ball in the hole. All the potential in the world was there.

But even when his knee had healed, all that potential could not be translated into performance. Kenny would go up for a sensational rebound—it would bring me right to my feet—and then I would not hear from him for five minutes. Sometimes it seemed like he was a lamppost at the outer perimeter of the action.

He was a hard worker and did everything we asked of him. I'd plead with him, "Show me something, Kenny, show me anything of that potential I know you have." He'd say he would but still nothing would happen.

For a while we thought he was afraid of the physical contact or that like Charlie Paulk he was not aggressive enough. At six-foot-seven and 220 pounds, he didn't have a lot of weight to throw around, and he was the type of forward who would get the job done with finesse rather than with muscle. He didn't shy away from contact, however, and in practice he could be very aggressive.

But he couldn't do it when the whistle blew and a real game began. We tried all kinds of psychology. We started him. We put him in when we were far behind. We put him in when we were way ahead. We put him in during close games. We tried everything, hoping to find the key to unlock all that talent. In the meantime, we were paying Kenny regular installments on his million-dollar contract.

In situations like this, it's easy for the coach to blame himself. I had a player at BC who I thought had more potential than Driscoll, Austin or anyone else I had recruited. But when I put the kid into a game, he couldn't do the job. I used to ask myself: *What did I do wrong with this kid, am I scaring him or something?* But after I left BC he played under two other coaches and he still couldn't do the job. Ironically, the pressure to win may have a kind of reverse effect on some people, causing them to tighten up and lose because they're afraid of losing.

I still don't know what the problem was in Kenny Durrett's case. The most likely explanation is that he had been inhibited by his injuries. Even when the physical problem is solved, a player may be apprehensive and have trouble regaining his confidence—as when a baseball player has been beaned and then has trouble digging in at the plate and batting aggressively. In basketball, a player whose legs are not sound may tend to ease off, especially when jumping, because of a fear that his knee may give out or that he'll be injured again.

In some cases, however, the reasons for this unrealized potential are harder to identify. It may be that as some people rise from one competitive level to the next, they look around one day, gulp, and say, "What am I doing here? I'm out of my league." And even though they may be able to compete physically or mentally at the job, they tighten up psychologically, fearing they will fail. When that happpens they often do fail.

I recall hearing the story of a high jumper who had never cleared the bar at six-foot-six, even though his coach was convinced he had the potential to reach that level. One day, at practice, the coach set the bar at six-six but told the boy it was at six-five.

The high jumper leaped over the bar.

"See," said the coach, showing the kid the setting. "The bar was set at six-six. You can do it."

The kid never high-jumped again. He had been willing to compete at a six-foot-five level, but no higher. I would not be surprised if there are people in nonathletic fields for whom this also may be true: consciously or unconsciously, they want to go so high, and no higher.

I remember a Brooklyn Dodger pitcher of the 1950's, Billy Loes, who once said he never wanted to be a twenty-game winner. He said he was satisfied with winning fifteen games a year. "When you win twenty," he said, cogently enough, "they expect you to go on winning twenty. If you win only eighteen the next season, you're a bum."

There's no doubt the pressure is there. I discovered it at Boston College. If you finish in first place one season and come back with the same team and finish second, you're not a bum, exactly, but people are disappointed. Penn State football coach Joe Paterno once put it this way: "It has to bother you when you do well and people expect more. You lose one or two games in a season and people ask what happened . . . 'What the hell went wrong?' That's ludicrous. That's crazy. You try to keep your perspective about it, but it's bound to warp your outlook. It's the mentality of the whole country. You can't lose."

Some people have suggested that players may fail because they're overpaid. They *are* paid more money than most of us ever dreamed of, and some may not be able to handle sudden wealth. But the argument that they "don't deserve" so much money is a hard one to defend. When pitcher Vida Blue was asking $100,000 from the Oakland A's after his rookie season, there were estimates that he could attract ten to fifteen thousand *additional* fans to every game he pitched. With thirty pitching starts, he could easily be responsible for putting 300,000 fans in the seats in addition to the regular attendance. Why shouldn't he get thirty-three cents for each of them?

From a coaching point of view, I had no objections to the rookies' getting all that money. If I was overpaid, why not them? But what I hated to see was a kid getting a no-cut contract. I used to tell Joe, "Let's sweeten the pot and give him more money if he'll sign a contract without a no-cut clause."

We were willing to guarantee payment of the full contract amount even if the player was cut. But every top draft pick we signed insisted—or his agent insisted—that he have a no-cut.

The no-cut contract hurts a team. If a high draft choice doesn't work out, he still occupies a spot on the bench for three years. Since every team is limited to twelve men, the no-cut player is taking up a valuable spot that might otherwise be filled by a player with more promise.

And the no-cut also hurts a player, as far as I'm concerned. He'll say, "Even though I have a no-cut, I've got pride. I'm going to be trying all the time." And I'm sure that he's sincere.

But he's forgetting the human element. In any competitive struggle, the guy who's fighting for his job is going to work harder and longer than the guy whose job is secure.

Let's say there are two NBA players with equal talent. One of the two has a no-cut contract, the other does not. Unconsciously or consciously, it seems to me, the kid with the no-cut is going to work a little less intensely because he knows that his job is secure, no matter what he does. If they play head-to-head against each other, the kid without the no-cut is going to hang in there a little longer than the kid with the no-cut. The no-cut contract dilutes the hunger that often makes great ballplayers.

Kenny Durrett had a world of talent but just couldn't translate it to performance. Many others lacked the talent in the first place. Every year we would draft or pick up as free agents a dozen or so rookies, hoping there might be a sleeper among them. Every club hopes to pick up somebody cheaply in the later rounds who might help the cause. For most players picked after the second round, however, the chances of playing in the NBA are slim. Of two hundred or so, two or three at the most will make an NBA team.

But hope, as they say, springs eternal. Each summer, at our camp for rookies, I would have to tell most of our draftees and free agents that they didn't have the talent.

It was easy when I had a kid who was a bad-ass. But nearly all of them, desperate to make the team, would say and do all the right things. They would try anything to soften me up—run laps after practice, anything. They wouldn't make a false step. They hadn't done a thing wrong, but one day I would have to call them in and tell them they were through.

I tried to be candid. "In my opinion," I'd tell them, "I don't think you can play at this level." But I would add: "Don't take that as gospel. Maybe you can get someone else to see talent that I don't see."

We might talk for a while and then I would usually tell them, "If you get a shot at another team, take it. But if the next guy tells you what I'm telling you, you have to look at the handwriting on the wall. Don't kill yourself and screw up your life for the next three or four years by trying to hang on here and there. Go out and find what you want to do with the rest of your life."

One year I cut all but four of the rookies. I called them into my office. "I've seen enough in you," I told them, "to invite you to come back with the veterans to our regular pre-season camp. But I want you to know what you're up against. There are four of you, plus the veterans coming back, so there will be seven or eight guys fighting for the one spot that's open." I paused to let this sink in. "I want you to know what the odds are. They're very slim. You could be wasting your time. If you have some other opportunity in another career, my suggestion is to take it. But if you want to take a last shot, you can come back."

Two of the four came back. But even though I had tried to prepare them, they were shattered when I had to cut them.

I couldn't blame them for trying to hang on. Ever since high school, people had been telling them how great they were and they had been dreaming about becoming rich young pros. I could understand why they would struggle to keep the dream alive.

Looking back, I'm amazed at how few individuals and teams ever make it in pro sports. Competition decrees that every year the losers outnumber the winners by twenty to one in the standings, by hundreds to one in the draft. Hating to lose as much as I do, I'm coming to realize that losing is the fate of almost everyone in one way or another, even those with talent, brains and desire.

With Durrett, our number one draft choice, out for most of the season with his injured knee, we began my third season at Cincinnati—1971–72—with much the same team as the previous year. Archibald and Van Lier were in the backcourt, Lacey at center, Van Arsdale and Johnny Green at the corners. We had obtained a promising rookie forward, Nate Williams, in a special hardship draft, and we had sent Charlie Paulk to Chicago in exchange for guard-forward Matt Guokas.

Late in October Darrall Imhoff, our backup center, broke an ankle. We were not intending to use Imhoff that much. But now, if anything happened to Lacey, we would be without a competent center. In the NBA that's like walking down an alley full of thieves without a weapon.

We called around, looking for a backup center. When the other teams know you're desperate, everyone tries to hold you up. Chicago offered us Jim Fox, a dependable backup center. But in exchange they wanted Norm Van Lier.

I agonized over that trade for days. I needed the center, I told myself. And on paper, with Tiny Archibald now showing that he could be an All-Star guard, Norman was expendable. Tiny could do almost everything that Norman could do and he was a much better scorer. If we traded Norman, Tiny would have the chance to run the team and multiply his skills. Tiny seemed to be coming out of his shell, and there is an old theory in the NBA that you can't have two guards on the floor at the same time who like to handle the ball.

Still, I didn't want to lose Van Lier. When he was in the game, he worked so hard that everyone else worked harder. And his unselfishness made everyone else unselfish.

I liked Norman off the court as well as on. He had been dating my older daughter Marie, who had met him when she came out from Boston for vacations. The coach can't get friendly with the players, but that shouldn't stop the coach's daughters.

Joe and I weighed everything and finally came to the conclusion that we should trade Van Lier for Fox. Fox turned out to be a dependable number two center for us. Van Lier went to Chicago and helped inspire the Bulls into playing what I thought was the best defense in the league by the following season.

But the Royals missed him—we missed his skills, and even more we missed his spirit. Before the season was over, I was convinced I should never have traded him. I should have taken the gamble that Lacey would stay healthy, which he did. And I should not have been concerned about inhibiting Archibald by playing him with another ball-handling guard. I would play three ball-handling guards before I would ever again give up a type like

Van Lier. He was not a super-talent. I could replace his ability. But I could never replace his attitude, his "heart," and what he did to make better players out of the four other guys playing with him.

After we traded Van Lier, some "nice guy" started a rumor that I had let Norman go because I didn't want a black man dating my daughter. That was a lie. As fine a player as I thought Norman was, I always thought he would have made a finer son-in-law.

From mid-December of 1971 on into January of '72 we lost eleven games in a row. I was going through an experience that had never happened to me before, one that doesn't happen to many coaches. It is almost unheard of in college to lose so many.

Then we lost a twelfth straight and a thirteenth. I began to ask myself, *Will we ever win again?* I looked at our schedule and wondered if it was possible to go from January through March without winning another game.

At all costs, I had to hide my worries and doubts from the players. I had to walk into the locker room before each game, be cheerful and say, "Now, hang in there, stick to our basic things and we can turn this around. Tonight is when we may blow somebody out of this building."

I knew that if they even suspected that their leader had his tail between his legs, it could be a wipe-out for the rest of the season. They would give up and I could see myself living through the nightmare of thirty-five or forty straight losses.

When we fell behind, I worried that the players would begin to think, The hell with this game. There's another one tomorrow night.

I knew the consequences of that attitude would be disastrous. Sometimes during a tennis match I would win the first set but be losing the second. Then I'd say to myself, *I could hang in there and bust my ass trying to win this set, but I probably won't win it anyway. I'll cool it and save myself for the third set.*

Well, the minute I accepted the idea that I was going to lose the set, I'd get wiped out—not only in the second set, but in the third set as well. The importance of sustaining your concentration and busting your ass in every game can hardly be overestimated.

Our next game was against the Bulls. We came from behind to tie the score at the buzzer. I thought we had the losing streak licked. But we lost in overtime, 108–104, our fourteenth straight defeat. We went to Buffalo for the next game.

That afternoon, before the game, I sat down with Max Jacobs. I thought I had to say something to him in explanation. I knew owners usually fire coaches when a team is losing and I wanted Max to know the option was open to him.

"Max," I said, "if we don't win this game tonight, I'm going to resign. The situation is that drastic."

Max said he wouldn't accept my resignation and he assured me he wanted me to stay. He told me he felt progress had been made in building up a nucleus of young players. Improvement in the won-lost column would come soon enough. I was relieved. Despite the stress of losing, I had no desire to leave the team in such bad times.

That night in Buffalo, the game went into overtime again. But this time Sam Lacey threw in the winning basket and we won, 109–107. The worst fourteen games of my life were behind me.

"Winning is getting to be monotonous," I said to the reporters in the clubhouse.

John Green topped me. He said, "I never thought I'd be glad to see a one-game winning streak."

Winners make jokes and it was nice to hear them again.

We finished that 1971–72 season winning thirty and losing fifty-two. Still, I thought we now had a team that needed only experience and two or three more good players to reach the playoffs. Even though we had lost more games each year, I felt that we had built a young, promising team from an old one that had been going nowhere.

I had fulfilled my three-year contract with Max. I still wasn't financially independent; my $100,000 a year had been invested in an equity market that was on its way down. But I had decided that I definitely would not come back to Cincinnati for the 1972–73 season, even though I had the option to do so if I wished.

I was homesick for my family and friends in Worcester, and I found living and competing in Cincinnati depressing, playing our games before small crowds in that old building. Whatever progress I thought I had made as a coach in building a nucleus of young players, I knew I had not saved the day at the box office.

Joe Axelson and I had been urging Max to move the team out of Cincinnati. He had offers to move to either San Diego or Kansas City–Omaha. We told him that Cincinnati had proved in good years and in bad years, with superstars and without superstars, that it would not support a pro basketball franchise.

Near the end of the season, Max told me he planned to sell the team to a group in Kansas City. The team, to be renamed the Kings, would play most of its home games in a new building in Kansas City and the rest in Omaha. Max knew I wanted to quit at the end of the season, but he asked me to stay one more year. He pointed out that it wouldn't look good, to the new fans or the new owners, if the so-called name coach didn't accompany the team.

I thought about the unfinished business of turning the team around and considered another year with a six-figure salary. The decision wasn't difficult. Once again, I said yes.

# THE MAKING
# OF A
# SUPERSTAR

I had always known that I was part of the entertainment business—as an NBA player and now as an NBA coach. As a player I could simply go out there, play as well as I could, and know I had done my job of entertaining the fans, especially if we won. Now, as a coach, I had to expand my responsibilities in the field of entertainment. I had to think not only about how to win but how to draw people into the arena. I made speeches, attended social affairs, and did a lot of promotion that had not been required of me as a player or as a college coach.

In the spring of 1972 Joe Axelson and I spent a lot of time discussing how to build fan support in Kansas City and Omaha for the new team. For this season, we were in the new Midwest Division with Milwaukee, Chicago and Detroit. We were confident that Milwaukee would finish first, and we felt we didn't have the guns to beat out both Chicago and Detroit for second place and a spot in the playoffs. So the question was how to keep the interest of the fans when we wouldn't be in championship contention.

We decided that we would try to make Tiny Archibald a superstar who would do what real superstars are supposed to do: put bodies in the seats. During the previous season Tiny had not been picked for the All-Star team and he resented the slight intensely. He went wild in the last half of the season to prove that he was a legitimate All-Star. He scored fifty-five points one night against Portland, forty-nine against New York. He was nearly always good for thirty or forty against Atlanta because there was a rumor that the vote of Atlanta coach Richie Guerin had kept him off the All-Star roster. (Guerin denied the story.) Tiny finished the season second in scoring only to Jabbar. He averaged twenty-eight points a game, and by then there was no question he was an All-Star.

For this first season at Kansas City we decided to give the ball to Tiny as often as we could, within reason, and let nature take its course. From an attendance point of view, we would have a superstar who would draw fans for the new team. And from a basketball point of view, by letting Archibald go with the ball, we would be taking some of the scoring responsibility off our other younger players, giving them a year to gain more experience without pressure. After that year we would expect them to take some of the scoring load off Tiny's shoulders.

Grooming one player to carry the scoring burden for the team was contrary to my usual coaching philosophy of balanced team play. But in our particular situation we would win more games with Archibald as the focal point

of our offense. In this case, I think, good showmanship
and good basketball were synonymous. For one thing, a
team may have the flashiest star in the league, but if it
doesn't win reasonably often the star and the team are in
trouble. The fans and the writers are shrewd enough to
spot a team that is stupid enough to lose games for the
sake of some star's scoring average. I could never have
done that. Even if I could have convinced myself I should
do it, my competitive nature wouldn't have allowed me to.

One day a reporter asked me how important winning an
ordinary regular season game was to me. "Let me take an
extreme case," I told him. "Suppose someone called me
five minutes before a game and said he was holding a gun
at my wife's head. 'If you don't lose this game,' he tells me,
'bang, this gun goes off.' I would go out there wanting to be
sure I lost that game. But once the game began, I don't know
if I could stop myself doing everything necessary to win."

Later I told Missie I was only kidding. But after twenty-
five years of marriage she knows the way I am.

I laid out for Tiny what we planned to do. "You'll go
with the ball this season," I told him, "but keep in mind
that you want to keep the four other guys happy. They're
the ones who will be getting you the ball."

I suggested that he do something that I had done as a
ball-handling guard. "When you're coming down the floor
on a fast break, one of the open men may be the forward
who got the rebound or the guard who just dove for a
loose ball. Keep your eye on that guy. Even if he doesn't
have as good an opportunity for a shot as the other open

man, give him the ball. If you give him some of the sugar, he's going to go on working hard for you."

Tiny was coming more and more out of his shell, but he was still a reticent kid with me. He nodded and said he understood. I hoped so. I knew we were taking the risk that he would not be able to adjust when his big year was over.

Missie and I rented an apartment in Kansas City. But now that both our daughters were attending college in Boston, Missie spent much more time back in Worcester, coming out to Kansas City only occasionally. I worried even more about her being alone in that big house. And I did not care to be living alone. I like to be among small groups and I often prefer to be alone, reading or simply meditating. But I am not the kind of animal who likes living alone.

Yet even with these irritants, the season went well from the start. Our turnaround was now being reflected in the won-lost columns. At Christmastime we had a nineteen-won, seventeen-lost record. Tiny was leading the league in scoring, averaging better than thirty points a game. And he was remembering the other guys. He was leading the league in assists, too.

Midway through the season we traded Tom Van Arsdale. Tom had played well for us for three straight seasons. But he didn't have the physical power to make himself felt under the boards as a rebounder. We sent him to Philadelphia in exchange for the six-foot-ten John Block, the power forward we needed to help Lacey on our forward wall.

Tiny, at about an even six feet in his sneakers, was on his way to becoming the first player in NBA history to lead in scoring (thirty-four a game) and assists (eleven a game) in the same year. He scored more points than any NBA guard in history.

Becoming a superstar brought Tiny even further out of that shell. Now he was standing up and making speeches at banquets with a reasonable amount of assurance. He would, I suspected, never be comfortable making a speech, but he was now showing a lot more self-confidence in public than I had felt at the age of twenty-four.

He had also changed in other ways. He had become somewhat difficult for the front office to handle. Occasionally he didn't show up for affairs after promising that he would. He would take the phone off the hook and be unreachable for days.

Becoming a celebrity changes people, there can be no question about it. On one hand they begin to resent the pressures and responsibilities of their new position—the banquets, the autographs, the repetitive questions. On the other hand, their egos enjoy the constant attention, and when their star fades they will miss some of the very things they resented. To expect a kid like Tiny to come out of a Bronx ghetto and be put on a pedestal as a sports idol and not change was being unrealistic. But we worried about some of the changes we were seeing. "I hope we're not turning this nice kid into a spoiled monster," I said to Joe one day.

We didn't keep our pre-Christmas pace, but we finished the 1972–73 season with a 36–46 record, the best since my first year at Cincinnati. I was learning that success in this business is relative. Five years earlier I might have felt a slight contempt for a coach and a team this far below .500. Now a 36–46 record was a sign of progress, a sign that we had turned the team around.

The year at Kansas City had been happy in a lot of other ways. The media gave us excellent support. And our attendance, compared to the previous year in Cincinnati, showed the biggest one-year jump of any NBA team in history.

I had not thought very often about my earlier resolution to coach only three seasons in the NBA. I was still hungry for success and unwilling to give up just because the job of turning the team around had taken a little longer than we planned. Competition creates an appetite for more competition, especially when victory seems close at hand.

There were probably some good reasons why I should have sat down at the end of that season and considered packing it in. My stomach was still tied in knots half the time. The schedule and travel were wearing me down. I disliked living alone most of the time and my wife was having to make the long commute from Kansas City to Worcester and back. My daughters were at an age when they might soon leave home to establish careers or families of their own. But the success of the Kings made my problems seem smaller.

If someone had mentioned quitting, I'm sure I would have voiced many of the same fears I had felt when I left Boston College: *What am I going to do in Worcester? I can always make a living, but what about that competitive*

*urge? What kind of withdrawal symptoms would I face?*
*Would I have those nightmares again?*

I'm sure I would have concluded that everyone has to follow his drum and that my drum was still competition.

# THE
# RUSSIANS
# ARE COMING

In March of 1973, before the season was over, I got a call from an old friend in New York, Ray Lumpp, who was then an official of the Amateur Athletic Union.

The AAU had arranged for a Soviet basketball team to come to the U.S. in April for a six-game tour. The team would be basically the same one that had won the Gold Medal in the 1972 Olympics at Munich, taking it away from the U.S. for the first time ever. The Soviet-American meeting at Munich had been fraught with controversy. Time ran out with the Americans ahead by one point. Then an official came out of the stands and allowed the last three seconds of the game to be replayed two different times. On the second replay the Russians scored a goal and won the game.

With that kind of background, I am sure the AAU saw an opportunity to make some money with an exciting tour —matching a team of Americans against the Russian team that had beaten us. Al McGuire, the coach at Marquette, was asked to recruit and coach the team.

Then the NCAA, which supervises college athletics, stepped into the picture. It had been feuding with the AAU for years and now saw a chance to win a point or two. The NCAA ruled that no college player or coach could participate in the games against the Russians. This ruling, however foolish, was within the power of the NCAA—they could declare any coach or player who participated ineligible for college competition. So the AAU was looking for a coach uninvolved in college coaching and was hoping to recruit a team from graduating seniors, who were beyond the reach of the NCAA.

So the AAU turned to the big bad pros and Ray Lumpp asked if I would coach the team. My first impulse was to say no. If I couldn't use college stars like Bill Walton (who was then a junior) and David Thompson (a sophomore), I thought I might have a lot of difficulty putting together a representative team to play the Olympic champions. I didn't want to end up having to go down to the Kansas City schoolyards and look for kids who could dunk the ball. I told Ray I would call him in a few days with a firm answer.

Still, the more I thought about coaching the American team, the more exciting and appealing it seemed. For one thing, I had always regretted not being able to play in the Olympics. Now I had the chance, as a coach, to represent my country and I liked the whole red-white-and-blue idea.

I agreed to take the job with two provisions. The first was that I have final approval on choosing players (according to rumor, Olympic coaches had sometimes been required to take players they didn't want). The second provision was that I pick my assistants. I wanted Draff

Young from the Kings and my old coach at Holy Cross, Buster Sheary. The AAU said fine.

Our first game would be on April 29 in Los Angeles at the Forum. I had only four weeks to find ten players willing to take two weeks out of school at the end of their senior year and then to prepare them to face the Russians. For the next two and a half weeks I was on the phone solidly, running up a bill of close to a thousand dollars, talking to players, coaches and agents.

At the last minute, the NCAA was forced to rescind its ban on underclassmen under pressure from Congress. Now we could use Bill Walton, if we could find him (he was always going off on a motorcycle to the mountains), and other underclassmen if we could persuade them to play.

But the job was still not easy. From most of the seniors on our top-priority list I got all kinds of excuses. One suddenly disappeared into a hospital; several said they were too busy or were taking final exams. In one case we made special arrangements with the dean of a university to postpone a boy's exams, but the player never showed up anyway.

Some of the excuses may have been legitimate. But I'm sure that in many cases their agents were telling the kids not to play. These players were expecting to be drafted in the first round by a pro team, but if they played poorly for us, they might not be picked in the first round and lose out on as much as half a million dollars. Financially, they may have been smart to duck the series. But I couldn't help thinking that I was seeing another manifestation of the selfishness that recruiting and big-money contracts have induced in kids with athletic talent.

When underclassmen were involved, we called their college coaches. One coach came straight to the point. "What's in this for us?" he asked.

When he learned there was nothing—we were all working free except for expenses—he said, "Well, I'll talk to the kid and call you back."

He never called back. Draff called again and reached one of his assistants, who said, "Oh, we talked to the kid and he's not interested."

Several months later we talked to the player himself and learned that the coach had never even mentioned our invitation.

I knew why some coaches didn't return our calls. They didn't want their sophomores or juniors getting national TV exposure against the Russians. An NBA or ABA team might notice a good performer and lure him away with an offer of big money. I suppose I couldn't really blame the coaches. They had to protect their meal tickets. If everyone else was being selfish, why shouldn't they?

On the other hand, I was receiving calls from agents of kids who were hoping to be drafted in maybe the second or third rounds. Those agents wanted their kids to play, hoping the exposure would get a team interested enough to pick their players higher in the draft. I didn't turn them down outright. But I stayed on the phone, trying to round up the best players.

It wasn't until about April 20—nine days before the first game—that I had a team I was reasonably satisfied with. The centers were Bill Walton and his backup center at UCLA, Swen Nater. For the backcourt we had Ernie DiGregorio of Providence, George Karl from North Carolina, Jim Oxley of Army and Tommy Henderson from

Hawaii. The forwards were Minnesota's Ron Behagen, Syracuse's Fred Saunders, St. Joseph's Pat McFarland and the North Carolina All-American, Bobby Jones.

In the week we had to get ready for the first game, I thought our biggest problem would be adjusting to the international rules on fouling. Under these rules, if you were fouled in the act of shooting, you got two shots. If you were fouled any other time, you only got the ball out of bounds. The Russians used the foul as a defensive weapon. When an opponent got the ball to a player close to the basket, they would foul him before he could shoot. As a result, opposing teams had to settle for the tougher outside shot. (This fouling rule was later changed and now is similar to our college regulations.)

Still, we had a lot of advantages. On offense, the Russians were deliberate, direct and unimaginative. Like most European players, they were generally weak in dribbling and passing. We thought that if we played aggressive defense we could pressure them into making mistakes. On offense, we decided to do a lot of running, hoping to get downcourt and into position to shoot before the Russians could foul.

I told Draff and Buster that I didn't want any emotional, patriotic appeals to the kids—at least not for this first game, which was generating tremendous publicity in Los Angeles. Using my own feelings as a barometer, I figured we were keyed up enough as it was. With all the talk about that loss in Munich, I was afraid that the team might be keyed too high.

But we did do one thing in the propaganda department. We had clipped a photo from *Sports Illustrated* that showed the Russians, after that victory at Munich, drinking from champagne bottles in their locker room. We just posted it on the bulletin board in the locker room without comment and left it there all week.

The first game was scheduled for a Sunday afternoon in Los Angeles. The day before the game the Russians were taken on a three-hour tour of Disneyland. During the next two weeks, they kept telling interviewers that the amusement park was the most impressive thing they had seen in the United States. When I heard about the visit I told Missie, who would be with us during the tour, "It's too bad they didn't walk them around for three hours on Sunday morning."

Both Missie and I, veterans of some twenty years of so-called "big games," were impressed by all the trappings and the atmosphere of international competition. There were flags all around the arena, bunting, flower girls, then the playing of the national anthems of the two countries. During "The Star-Spangled Banner" Buster Sheary was so proud that the buttons seemed to be ready to pop right off his coat. Looking at him, I came close to tears.

Early in the game Bill Walton injured himself. He had played only thirteen minutes and he would not return for the rest of the series. But we ran our fast breaks well and played an aggressive full-court defense that forced the Russians, as I had hoped, into errors. They looked even more flatfooted than usual, perhaps because of all that tramping through Disneyland. Even without Walton, we won easily, 83–65.

The next night we played at the San Diego Sports Arena. This time we looked tired. We didn't run on offense, we didn't come out to harass them on defense. As in all the games on the tour, the Russians shot well and their stolid physical types gave us a good going-over under the boards. The rough play on both sides was a warning of things to come. They won, 78–76, but they should have won by more.

We flew to Albuquerque for the third game. I had the feeling that this one would decide who would win the six-game series. Our team had been reduced to nine men through injuries, and although we had sent out a call for reinforcements they wouldn't arrive in time for this game. Everyone seemed down after the physical beating the Russians had given us in San Diego.

When I had asked Buster Sheary, who was now in his sixties and had been out of coaching for some years, to assist me with this team, some people had said, "Isn't that nice, you took your old college coach." But I knew that Buster had a lot to contribute. When I played for him at Holy Cross, I had learned a few bad habits from him. I had seen him smack steel lockers with his bare fists to emphasize a point. Once he even banged his head against a wall. Buster knew how to make his point: If you don't want something to hurt, it won't hurt. *Bang!* And if you want to win badly enough, no one can keep you from winning. *Bang!*

Many people believe that today's kids would never go for that kind of pep talk—that they would laugh such a coach out of the room. But I was willing to give Buster a chance.

Before the game in Albuquerque I talked for a few minutes with the players and then I asked him to go over the defensive assignments. I knew full well, of course, what would occur. Buster, up against the Russians, wasn't going to stop with the defensive assignments.

He took only about six or seven minutes. He got to waving the flag and saying all the things that today's sophisticated kids are supposed to laugh at. I looked around the room and I could see that nearly all the players—these confident college All-Americas—were being moved by Buster's speech. I had to leave the room, fearing I might break down myself. The team almost took the doors off the hinges on their way out of the room. The game was over in about twelve minutes. I believe we had a twenty-four-point lead at the half. I don't think a team could get up much higher than they were that day.

By contrast, I noticed the Russians seemed to have no peaks and valleys. They seemed to play each game at about the same emotional level. It seemed that their coach just sat on the bench, dispassionately pushing buttons and the players would get up and do exactly what he told them to do. From a strict coaching point of view, I envied him. His players seemed to work hard all the time and play up to their potential. For a coach, this is what it is all about, getting your athletes to perform exactly as they are capable of performing and exactly as they are asked to perform.

We won the fourth game of the tour in Indianapolis and came to New York's Madison Square Garden ahead, three games to one. The Russians had the lead for most of the game and we seemed to have lost. Then, in the closing minutes, Jim Oxley made some alert steals and we tied the game. In overtime, Ernie DiGregorio put in some clutch hoops and we won.

We played for the last time in Baltimore on May 9. From an artistic point of view, the game was terrible. After six games in eleven days, players were getting on each other's nerves and there were a couple of near fights. They won the game but neither team played very well.

As I watched violence threaten in the closing minutes, I thought back to an incident in the second game, at San Diego. One of the Russians was intimidating our players and we were getting beat. I began to get angry. Then, following my lifelong instinct to dish it out when someone else has started it, I turned to Ron Behagen, who was sitting next to me, and I said, "Ron, I want you to go in there and decapitate that bastard."

Ron leaped up and reported into the game. A minute later, as he was running by the bench next to the Russian bad guy, he did his best to follow my orders literally. He suddenly lifted his elbow and threw it right at the Russian's head.

I am convinced that if the elbow had connected, the Russian's head would have rolled the length of the court. Fortunately, the player ducked. Ron got thrown out of the game.

Later, after we had shaken hands with the Russians and parted reasonably good friends, I told myself, *If Ron had killed that Russian, you would have had some explaining to do. That killer instinct of yours has taken you a long way, but this time it came close to starting World War Three.*

# WALKING AWAY

I felt a tremendous satisfaction after we had won the series against the Russians. Perhaps I had started to doubt my capabilities as a coach. I had always felt that I knew the game and could teach it; I knew I could handle the players. But after you go through four years of losing more often than you win, the experience has to affect you to some extent. The victory over the Russians was not only satisfying in itself, it acted as a healthy reinforcement to my confidence.

During the summer of 1973, shortly after the Russian series, I went to Europe to lecture on basketball to Spanish coaches. I brought Missie and my two daughters with me. Marie had graduated from college and Tish from a junior college. I thought a three-week tour of Europe would be a nice graduation present.

As the girls began to establish their own lives, I began to realize how little I had participated in normal family life during the years when they were growing up. Shortly after Missie and I were married, in 1950, I had become a pro player and within a few years I was a star. I was probably no different from many other athletes and a lot of other successful career men. I had become completely wrapped up in my career. Everything revolved around me and my thing. In sports, the time you have to make it is relatively short, so you give all your attention to succeeding and there is very little time left over for your family.

One night the previous summer I had visited Frank and Jean Ramsay in Louisville. Frank had been the famous "sixth man" on the Celtics, the guy who came off the bench so often in close games to push us ahead with three or four quick hoops.

During the evening the conversation turned to how many of our friends who had been athletes had gotten divorces in their late thirties and forties. Jean said that athletes' wives were often closer to the other players' wives than they were to their husbands. Many of them looked up to their husbands the way a fan would, putting them on a pedestal. And the athlete, traveling a lot and wrapped up in his own competitive career, didn't give the time to participating in normal family relationships.

Then the guy retired. He was passing out of the limelight and that was a difficult transition. He had to make adjustments in his outlook on life. And the wife had to get accustomed to a man who has come down from his pedestal. It was almost like starting all over again for each of them. Often they had built so little real foundation in the early years that they couldn't adjust to the new situation and the marriage crumbled.

Jean's theory made me think about my own family relationships. Missie had been the focal point of the lives of my daughters. I suppose I rationalized by thinking that I spent the summers with the family at camp. But even there I was busy teaching basketball and arranging all the activities. I had seldom participated in the customary family activities—picnics, helping with schoolwork, going out for an afternoon bike ride, and so on.

I had led my life without really thinking about slighting my family. I guess I assumed everything should revolve around me and my career. My thoughts were focused on my activities, my getting attention, my being successful. It troubled me to think that the selfishness I had seen in blue-chip high school stars, pampered All-Americas and millionaire pro players was not much different from my own selfishness. Like them, I had put my own ambitions first. Family and other personal relations came second.

But as the new season approached, the old itch to get back to competition returned. The Russian series had produced that addict's high of euphoria. The more I looked back on how much I liked Kansas City, the progress we had made at the gate, the rise of Tiny to superstardom, and the overall improvement of the team, the more I thought, *Hey, one more year, why not?*

We came back from Europe in September. A few weeks later, without thinking about much except the season ahead, I got into my car with Missie and drove to Kansas City for the start of the 1973–74 season.

At training camp I sat down and went through our change of strategy with Tiny Archibald. "This year we're going to have to spread out the offense," I told him. "You can't go on carrying it alone, and we have other guys who can put the ball in the hole. But you're still the leader and the playmaker, the guy who's going to have to know when to shoot and when to pass off."

Tiny agreed. And when I made it clear to the rest of the team that we would run a more team-oriented offense this season, I got no arguments.

In practice I saw the running offense, the control of the boards and the aggressive defense that I had been working to instill in the team for the past four years. Sam Lacey had come a long way. On a good night he could compete on fairly even terms with any center in the league.

At guard we had Tiny. Even in his new role, he could not be stopped with any consistency. Early in the season, we would add to our backcourt scoring potential by trading for Jimmy Walker, the former Providence All-American. And our number two draft choice, Mike D'Antoni, soon showed that he was an excellent ball-handler.

Our number one draft pick, Ron Behagen, was the scrappy forward who had impressed me against the Russians. Kenny Durrett showed only flashes of the brilliance we had expected from him, but Behagen made up for any disappointments I felt, soon winning a starting forward spot from Kenny. Another forward, Nate Williams, had superb quickness, and John Block gave us rebounding power.

All in all, this seemed to be a team with more potential than any I had coached in the NBA.

When the pre-season games began, Missie—still unhappy and lonely in Kansas City—went back to Worcester. Commuting was more difficult for her than it had been when we were in Cincinnati, so I faced being alone in our apartment for most of the season.

The pure ridiculousness of the situation really hit me: my wife, my daughters, my friends, my home, were in Worcester. I had not spent the time with my family that I should have during the past twenty-odd years. Now my daughters were twenty and twenty-two. Any day a career choice or a marriage could take them away from the house for good. What were my priorities, even if I was on the verge of coaching a winning team? Was winning or money so important that I should be miles away from my family and friends for months at a time?

I went to Joe Axelson and told him I wanted to leave. He asked me to stay until the end of the season. My sudden leaving could disrupt the team. I had never walked out on a contractual obligation before and I didn't want to do it now. Reluctantly, I stayed.

We opened the 1973–74 season against Chicago. During the game the Bulls' Tom Boerwinkle stepped on Tiny's foot. After the game, which we lost, Tiny said the foot was all right, but during the next few weeks he had trouble with it and complained that it bothered him. Medical tests revealed an injury that would put him out for the rest of the season.

The loss of our scoring champ hurt us. We had to regroup and learn how to play without our best playmaker. The team responded well, Lacey and Williams in particular. We weren't playing badly, but we weren't winning, either. Shortly after Tiny's departure, we went through a six-game losing streak.

After each loss I would go into the clubhouse and try to

encourage the players. Then I would meet the press, answering questions about our latest performance. I often recalled something Joe Lapchick once said. One year his St. John's team had lost in the finals of a tournament. At the post-tournament dinner for the participants, Joe was asked to say a few words. "I was told many years ago," he said, "that it doesn't matter whether you show up after you win. But be damned sure you show up after you lose."

Of course, he was right. I began to realize, however, that while everyone may seem to love you when you are a winner, some people are envious enough to feel a little joy when a former winner loses.

Sometimes I got the impression a questioner was needling me. As I began to get angry I told myself, *You answered all their questions when they were writing puff pieces about you. Now answer the questions when things aren't going as well.*

The worst part of showing up after a loss would be having to attend the after-game parties that owners give for season ticket-holders. I would stand at those parties, a drink in my hand, answering the same questions that have been asked at sports banquets from the beginning of time. I'd smile and answer the questions while thinking to myself, *You may be overpaid for coaching, but you're sure earning your salary right now.*

These "rewards" for losing were not new. I had been learning to deal with them for four seasons. But it didn't seem to get any easier. Now, in my fifth season, losing and all that went with it made me more miserable than ever. There was a temptation to give up and say, *Oh, hell, these guys are not ready to do it, or they may never be ready to do it, but I'm stuck with them, so I'll just sit back, collect my money and stop worrying.*

I envied other coaches—in fact, anybody—who could adopt that attitude. But I thought that if you sat back and took defeats with equanimity, it may be fine for your health but you would not be as concerned and competent a coach or salesman or executive. If you have a job that requires constant attention and emotional dedication, I am afraid, you have the choice in our competitive society of playing it cool and doing only half a job or agonizing like hell and perhaps running yourself into the ground.

For the first time in my life, I was feeling jealous when I saw another coach who was doing well. I found myself thinking, *I hope he slips a little.* That surprised me because, as far as I could recall, I had never felt any jealousy toward anyone during my career. When I retired from the Celtics, I remember being a little surprised and hurt when others on the team said in the newspapers that they wanted to win another championship to prove they could win without Cousy. I detected some jealousy there that I hadn't previously suspected. But now, ten years later, I began to understand why there might have been some jealousy and to see why I had never felt it before. As a player I had always thought of myself as being on top, the best in the game. From that view, I couldn't see anyone to be jealous of. Now, as a coach looking up from the bottom of the league, I found jealousy came easier.

It is only natural as you get older to begin to analyze yourself as I was doing. It had been five years since I wrote out my resignation at Boston College. I had left because winning games only seemed to push me into wanting to win more. Now, after learning what it was like not to win very often, I was questioning my behavior on an even deeper level. How important was competition, anyway? How long could you go on, proving yourself game after game, aiming for a kind of perfection that is always just around the corner?

After all, there are so many areas of life in which competition doesn't apply. Should a man compete with or against his family? Should Americans devote billions of dollars to preserving the boast that they have never lost a war? Does the hardest competitor have the happiest life or does he just drive himself to an early grave?

Perhaps I had put too much stock in competition. If I had to do it over again, I told myself, I would look for a better balance between the competitive and noncompetitive sides of life, giving more time and attention to my family, and to noncompetitive pursuits—reading, reflecting, helping others.

These are not surprising conclusions—many intense, competitive people have had the same thoughts. But doing something about them is another matter. Here I was worrying about my family and my own well-being and I was fifteen hundred miles from home, locked into the same pressure-filled situation that I had alternately loved and hated for years.

No matter how often we lost or what second thoughts I was having about my life, the killer instinct was still alive within me. Early in the season Chicago's Jerry Sloan was beating us in a game with one hoop after another. Jerry is a fighter, the kind of player every coach loves. He plays a very physical game. One of our backup guards, Dick Gibbs, was playing against him.

I knew Sloan's history: if you needled him, he often became upset to the point of losing his effectiveness. As Sloan and Gibbs were running by our bench, I yelled, "Gibbs, the next time that son of a bitch pushes you, tear his damn head off!"

Sloan heard me—I could see him turn red with anger. During a free throw, he came toward our bench and gave me an upward motion with his fist. I waved him off with a show of contempt.

Just as I had hoped, he was so angry that he didn't get a hoop for the rest of the game and we beat the Bulls. Afterwards, I felt a little ashamed of what I had done. A coach shouldn't be in the business of baiting opposing players. As soon as the game ended, I went over to apologize. Jerry came at me and it took three guys to restrain him. Which was just as well, since Jerry is younger and bigger than I am. But I knew if I had to bait Sloan or anyone else the next night in order to win a game, I would do it.

We didn't win often during the first couple of months of that 1972–73 season, losing twelve of our first eighteen. I was going two or three days without a full meal, existing on small breakfasts and sandwiches.

One night I am sitting alone in the hotel room. I have been coming to this city as coach and player for almost twenty-five years. I can call any one of a dozen or more people for dinner. But I don't.

That night, after losing another game I come back to

the hotel, no appetite for even a sandwich, but I am wound up tighter than a spring. I go up to my room, close the door and open my suitcase. Inside are two miniature bottles of Scotch, the kind airlines give away. I take out the two bottles and pour them into a water glass. While I look over the statistics of the game, I drink from the glass, emptying it. When I feel the whiskey starting to work, I take off my clothes and sleep comes quickly.

The next morning I look at myself in the mirror. I think about the Scotch and decide it is not a healthy habit. I have never been much of a drinker, and I am not really concerned that I am going to become an alcoholic. But if we go on losing, will I start needing two glasses of Scotch, then three, before I am able to sleep?

The face in the mirror is lined and drawn. Yesterday a friend told me I looked exhausted.

Late in November, just before Thanksgiving, we lost to Philadelphia at home in Kansas City, 109–103. After the game, I was particularly depressed. Even without Tiny, I thought we should have beaten Philadelphia at home.

The next night, Thanksgiving Eve, we played Philadelphia, this time in Omaha. Again we lost, 103–90.

At the final buzzer, I got up from the bench and started to walk across the floor to the dressing room. On the way, I made the decision that I would walk into the clubhouse and announce to the reporters that I was quitting.

# THE
# KILLER
# INSTINCT

**M**issie heard the news on the radio back in Worcester. She was shocked. Later she told someone it was the first snap decision I had ever made in my life.

It wasn't a snap decision, of course. Like Bill Flynn's phone call to me, telling me that Bobby Griffin couldn't come to Boston College, those two losses to Philadelphia were catalysts that brought me more quickly to decisions I would otherwise have made at a different time and place.

When I told Joe I was leaving, a few minutes after I told the reporters in the dressing room, I still felt bad about the contract. My old sense of obligation rose up. I promised Joe that if the owners insisted, I would stay on through the end of the season. The team was flying to Boston the next morning, but I got on a different plane and headed home to Worcester.

On Thanksgiving afternoon I had dinner with Missie and my daughters, the first time in a long while that we had been together for this holiday. But the dinner was spoiled for me by the promise I had made to Joe Axelson.

I knew he would be calling me with the owners' decision. I dreaded the possibility that I might have to go back to Kansas City. I told myself, *You should have said, "I'm quitting, that's it."*

The phone rang. It was Joe. He said, "Bob, I've got some bad news for you." My heart dropped—I didn't want to go back. Then he continued: "The owners have agreed to release you from your contract." I was puzzled about why Joe thought that was bad news. Apparently, he didn't think I really wanted to quit. But I thanked him, hung up, and enjoyed the rest of my dinner with a tremendous sense of relief.

Only a few months before, I had driven to Kansas City with high hopes for the new season. There had been disappointments with the team and more games to lose, but like the Griffin incident those past few months in Kansas City did not contain enough momentous events to explain my resignation. After dinner I sat in my study and did some contemplating about where I had been these past ten years as a coach and what had happened to me.

For the first time I really considered the idea that I was an addict, strung out on the need to compete and the need to win in whatever I did. The parallels were frightening. For thirty years I had devoted my life to making a regular connection with a game where I could enjoy the highs of proving myself the best. My habit wasn't illegal in itself, but if it was strong enough it could lead a man to lie and cheat. Like other habits, it took its toll over the years. The pressures of getting myself up for a game, of playing, of agonizing as a coach, had now driven me to the point where I had to withdraw.

And yet I knew I got my greatest kicks out of competing and winning. I don't have a steel-trap memory of past games and seasons, nor do I care to sit around at night and rehash how the Celtics won a championship. Most of the trophies I won are stored away in my basement. But I have very sharp memories of particular plays and winning moments; they are as clear in my mind as if they were happening this minute. Those moments had helped me to see a meaning in my life—they had given me the momentary sensation that I knew what it was all about. And I knew that whatever happened I would crave more of those flashes of euphoria that came when I put the ball in the hoop against a great opponent or won when the circumstances said I should lose. It would be difficult to live without competition—perhaps almost as difficult as living with it.

By now I had come to the conclusion that I had a choice. I could try to absorb a loss without such agony, learning to compete without making winning and losing everything. Somehow I felt this went against my nature. Or I could live and die with the scoreboard, straining to get every ounce out of myself and my players. But perhaps that was a killing game that would end in a nervous breakdown or worse.

I thought about Jerry Lucas, the man who had irritated me by considering basketball a nine-to-five job and going through his career giving 80 percent of his talent. I could agree intellectually that the Jerry Lucases of the world have the wiser approach to life. But in me the competitive drive runs too deep. I still couldn't imagine myself as an 80 percent competitor, in basketball or in anything else. So far in my life I had to give everything of myself to competition. Or I had to walk away when the pressures I put on myself got too great.

But now, at least, I was home. Missie and my daughters were glad to see me. They had stuck by me even though it seemed they had often given more than I had been willing to give in return. When you compete at the 100 percent level, you have neither the time nor the energy for your family. I resolved to find much more time now that I was back.

When my thoughts turned to tomorrow, however, I began to get a queasy feeling. A knot tightened in my stomach. Tomorrow, for the first time in almost thirty seasons, there would be no basketball game for me to get up for, plan for, compete in, and win or lose.

I felt disoriented. I began to sweat. My mind was made up to accept a life at a less intense competitive level. But the emotional side of me was rebelling. Perhaps, I thought, these are the first withdrawal symptoms.

I sat there in the study for five or six hours, becoming more and more depressed. I went to bed thinking, *What have I done?*

I woke up the next morning feeling much better. The knot had loosened. During the next few weeks I began to work on a whole series of new projects. It was difficult for me to slow down, but I found that as long as I kept busy I was reasonably happy.

My addiction is still with me. I crave competition and the highs of winning. In my business life I still want to be as perfect as is within my power. The killer instinct that I was cultivating in that Los Angeles hotel room in 1963 still rears its head. In a friendly golf or tennis game, I feel the coils tightening and I think, *I am going to win. I am going to succeed. No Frank Selvy or anyone else is going to stop me.*

But I'm no longer so proud of the killer instinct. It may be the drive that makes a superstar in sports, sells a product or wins a war. But it can do more than blow away an opponent. It can kill the moral sense, the happiness of a family, even the man himself. It is not an instinct I can get rid of. It is something I must live with as best I can.